THE
DEAN'S DAUGHTER.

THE
DEAN'S DAUGHTER.

A PLAY, IN FOUR ACTS.

BY

F. C. PHILIPS & SYDNEY GRUNDY.

LONDON:
TRISCHLER & COMPANY,
18, NEW BRIDGE STREET, E.C.
1891.

PRINTED BY
'THE HANSARD PUBLISHING UNION, LIMITED, LONDON;
AND REDHILL.

CHARACTERS.

Sir Henry Craven.

The Rev. Augustus St. Aubyn (afterwards Dean of Southwick).

Prince Balanikoff.

George Sabine.

Lord Ashwell.

Colonel Vandeleur.

Mr. Slark, ⎫ Tradesmen, Creditors of Mr. St.
Mr. Twentyman, ⎬ Aubyn.

First Guest.

Second Guest.

Valet.

Miriam St. Aubyn (afterwards Lady Craven), the Dean's daughter.

Mrs. Fortescue (her friend).

Lady Ashwell.

Mrs. Peel.

Elise (Lady Craven's maid).

OPINIONS OF THE PRESS
UPON
THE DEAN'S DAUGHTER,
BY
F. C. PHILIPS & SYDNEY GRUNDY.

Founded upon "The Dean and his Daughter," by F. C. Philips, and produced at the St. James's Theatre, October 13th, 1888.

THE TIMES.

"No mealy-mouthed adaptation from the French is put forth at the St. James's as an abstract and brief chronicle of English life. 'THE DEAN'S DAUGHTER' is the product of English brains, breathing in every line an English spirit."

DAILY TELEGRAPH.

"The best criticism of 'THE DEAN'S DAUGHTER,' a tale of modern life and manners, told by two exceedingly able and clever men— Mr. Sydney Grundy and Mr. F. C. Philips—is contained in the narration of it. All parts of the house in a remarkably demonstrative manner testified their warm approval. Nothing went amiss."

THE WORLD.

"'THE DEAN'S DAUGHTER' is full of novel and ingenious detail; its tone is alert and modern; and its dialogue, without any epigrammatic tawdriness, is nervous and natural. The character of the Rev. Augustus St. Aubyn, and the whole conception of the last act, are indubitably dangerous, their acceptance being secured by a triumph of tact—a triumph, let me add, in which I heartily rejoice. Neatest of all is the last moment of the play— a 'happy ending' in two senses. It is in the conception and preparation of such an effect that we recognise the born dramatist."

DAILY NEWS.

"A situation that is full of dramatic power, and is sustained throughout by a great play of passion, will move the spectators in spite of all drawbacks, and this was never more strikingly exemplified than in the progress of the really magnificent last act of the play of Messrs. Philips and Grundy. . . . Such qualities as these go far to explain the triumph of authors and management on Saturday evening; for triumph it was."

THE MORNING POST.

"The authors have shown so much skill in the arrangement of the incidents, and have furnished the dialogue with so many quaint conceits, shrewd bits of worldly wisdom, and daring paradoxes as smart as they are cynical, that the audience never appeared to experience a moment's doubt or dulness, but were kept interested and amused all the time. The impersonation of the heroine by Miss Olga Nethersole was certainly a remarkable performance both in force and feeling for so youthful a lady, richly deserving all the applause it received, which culminated in something like a triumph at the conclusion of the piece. Of its success there can be no doubt; it was decisive and unqualified, Mr. Barrington and Miss Nethersole receiving special compliments in addition to those ordinarily bestowed."

THE GLOBE.

"The piece obtained a complete hold upon the public, by whom it was received with enthusiasm; cheering more hearty or more sustained than attended the fall of the curtain has rarely been heard in a place of entertainment, all concerned in the representation, from the authors downwards, being included in the triumph to which they all contributed. The performance was, in the full sense of the term, interpretive. No sign of success was wanting.

REFEREE.

"The verdict of to-night was favourable from first to last."

THE PEOPLE.

"Briefly to sum up, the merits of the play, by its constructive skill and dramatic dialogue, the epigrammatic point which expedites rather than impedes the action, achieved unqualified success."

GRAPHIC.

"'THE DEAN'S DAUGHTER' must be pronounced an unequivocal success."

PALL MALL GAZETTE.

"The reception of the play was throughout enthusiastic, and we shall be surprised if Mr. Barrington has not secured a genuine success."

OPINIONS OF THE PRESS.

STAR.

"The house received play, players, and playwrights with the heartiest applause. Any attempt should be welcomed on the dramatist's part to break through the hollow optimism, the deadening worship of the comfortable and the palatable, which has always been the curse of English art, whether in the library, the picture gallery, or the playhouse. Such an attempt, and a fearless one, has been made by the authors of 'THE DEAN'S DAUGHTER,' a play taking its personages straight from life, planting them firmly on their feet, and putting in their mouths dialogue always racy, and sometimes even brilliant."

SPORTING TIMES.

"Mr. Rutland Barrington commenced his managerial career at the St. James's Theatre on Saturday night, with a drama by Messrs. Sydney Grundy and F. C. Philips. Go and see it, gentle reader; you will not be disappointed."

THE MORNING ADVERTISER.

"The play is well written, and contains some capital lines. Messrs. Grundy and Philips were called on and warmly applauded."

THE SCOTSMAN.

"The piece obtained a favourable reception, the actors and authors being called before the curtain."

SCOTTISH LEADER.

"The re-opening of the St. James's Theatre to-night was distinguished by the production of a powerful, well-constructed, and interesting play, and by the triumphant success achieved by a young and comparatively unknown actress. Miss Olga Nethersole, who played Miriam, won a triumph such as rarely falls to the lot of so young an artist. To great beauty of person and face, she adds true dramatic feeling, and her career can scarcely fail to be a brilliant one. The play, which was beautifully mounted, was an undoubted success, and the authors received an enthusiastic call."

THE SATURDAY REVIEW.

"Among writers who have recently come to the front, Mr. F. C. Philips holds high rank, and in the preparation of his book for the theatre Mr. Philips has had the advantage of Mr. Sydney Grundy's assistance. One situation is extremely ingenious; what has been done is to make Lady Craven appear a guilty woman in the eyes of her husband and father, who have suddenly and without her knowledge arrived at Nice, where she is staying. They suspect George Sabine as her lover; as a matter of fact the audience know that this is not so, and have just seen her dismiss him, admitting her affection for him, but securing his promise to leave Nice because the affection exists. How then is she to be compromised? It is done by causing a brutal Russian Prince, whom she has attracted, to find his way to her room through a window which he has bribed her maid to leave open, and make her call for help; thereupon Sabine overhears her and rushes to her aid through the open window, and after dealing with the Russian, receives her fainting in his arms; thus she is found, and the inference to be drawn is apparently obvious, though in truth it is utterly wrong."

EVENING POST.

"Miriam is a loyal-hearted maiden and true woman, and brave to the last. These qualities Miss Nethersole rendered with instinctive spontaneous fervour. Her voice had the ring of sincerity, her action was girl-like and unaffected. From the first act onward she was the heroine of the evening, and had the lead of the calls. The house expressed by long and continued applause its best wishes for Mr. Barrington's success."

MAN OF THE WORLD.

"The dialogue is so witty that to find a comparison for it I must go to France. It is as philosophical as Dumas and as light as Pailleron. The talk is good enough to be an acceptable excuse when it delays the action of the piece. The play, I am sure, would be as entertaining to read in print as it is on the stage; for it is a piece of sterling dramatic literature."

UNITED SERVICE GAZETTE.

"There can be no doubt as to the success of 'THE DEAN'S DAUGHTER.'"

THE COURT JOURNAL.

"The new play is smartly written and admirably played. Miss Olga Nethersole represented the Dean's daughter. Her graceful appearance, tender, sympathetic manner, and very expressive features admirably fitted her for the emotional part of Miriam. Her excellent performance was followed with the closest attention."

THE STAGE.

"The play is an able example of its class. Well conceived and highly wrought, sustained and often powerful in its interest, full of brilliant if stinging persiflage, 'THE DEAN'S DAUGHTER' is a drama of skilled workmanship. . . . . 'THE DEAN'S DAUGHTER' is a piece of stage-craft that shows the fashioning of a master."

THE DEAN'S DAUGHTER.

ACT I.

SCENE.—THE HALL AT THE VICARAGE AT OSSULSTON. (*Enter Mr. Slark, the butcher, and Mr. Twentyman, the grocer, of Ossulston, shown in by Mrs. Peel, the Vicar's housekeeper.*)

MRS. P.

Take a seat, please; Mr. St. Aubyn will see you directly.

(*Exit Mrs. Peel.*)

MR. S.

Well, Twentyman, what do you think of the look of things?

MR. T.

Don't like it at all, Slark. He owes me over twenty pounds, and from what I hear I'd be glad to take five bob in the pound.

MR. S.

Don't you wish you may get it? He was up at the County Court on Tuesday in a judgment summons. Gosling, the stationer, had supplied the old bloke with reams of paper and pints of ink to write a history of the county, and make his fortune. But Gosling couldn't prove no means, and the judge ordered the Vicar to pay by monthly instalments of four bob.

MR. T.

That means it'll take about five years to clear it off.

MR. S.

Jes' so. It don't look very smiling for us. What do *you* think? (*Sotto voce.*) Here he is.

(*Enter the Rev. Augustus St. Aubyn; gardening gloves and rake.*)

VICAR.

Ah, gentlemen! Delighted to see you! What a lovely day! I hope business is flourishing. I am always glad to hear that my neighbours are doing well; though Providence, in its inscrutable wisdom, has hitherto been pleased to decree that mine should be a hard lot, and has even on occasions gone so far as to deny me the kindly fruits of the earth.

MR. T.—(*Aside.*)

Topper the greengrocer's refused to serve him.

VICAR.—(*Continuing.*)

Still, I am ever delighted to hear of the prosperity of others. We must think of others, my dear friends, if we would be really happy.

MR. S.

We must think of ourselves sometimes, Vicar. Now, you've got into my ribs for a matter of thirty-five pounds.

VICAR.

Ha! ha! ha!

MR. T.

I don't see it's a very laughing matter.

VICAR.

I was only tickled at your ready wit. "Got into his ribs" from a butcher is very neat.

MR. S.

Never mind that, sir. What I want to know is, what you propose doing?

TWENTY.

Yes, Vicar, that's what we want to know—what you purpose doing?

VICAR.

My dear friends, when I have a definite proposition to make I shall lose no time in formulating it.

SLARK.

That won't do, Vicar. I ain't seen the colour of your money for nearly five months.

TWENTY.

No, nor I, Mr. St. Aubyn. I have nine children to bring up, and I must have my money.

VICAR.

Nine children! (*Aside.*) What terrible imprudences the lower orders commit. (*Aloud.*) You shall have your money, Slark. You shall have your money, Twentyman. But you will gain nothing by pressing me. Gosling tried that, and I dare say you have heard the result?

SLARK.

Well, I shan't serve you any more, and I shall see what my solicitor, Mr. Sledger, has to say in the matter.

TWENTY.

I call it obtaining goods under false pretences, and I mean to try what the law will do, if I have to spend ten pounds.

VICAR.

Pray sit down, Mr. Slark; you make me nervous in that attitude. (*Slark sits down.*) Thank you. I have had, my friends, for the last twenty years to struggle with the direst misfortunes that ever beset a scholar, a gentleman, and a divine.

SLARK.

That's no affair of ours.

VICAR.

Be good enough to bear with me. I have lost money. I have failed to obtain preferment. But a change—a vast change—is looming in the distance. Nay, I am wrong. It is not in the distance; it is close at hand.

TWENTY.

What do you mean, sir?

VICAR.

The Dean of Southwick is in *articulo mortis*. Perhaps you don't understand that, Twentyman? (*Twentyman looks bewildered.*) The Dean of Southwick is at the point of death. Dear Dr. Proby is one of my very oldest and best friends, but we must not repine: that is sinful.

SLARK.

Well, sir, if Dr. Proby do die he won't leave you nothing. He've got a wife and family of his own.

VICAR.

I may say at once that I have no expectations from my poor friend. But when it pleases Providence to remove the Dean, the Deanery still remains. Slark, it is in the highest degree probable that I may be transferred to another and wider sphere of usefulness: in other words, to the Deanery of South-wick.

TWENTY.—(*Astonished.*)

You don't say so!

SLARK.

I never heard a word of this before.

VICAR.

I am to-day expecting my old friend Sir Henry Craven, Her Majesty's Minister at Madrid, who is about to receive the Embassy at Constantinople. He tells me that the Deanery is as good as in my possession. The Deanery, Slark, carries with it fifteen hundred a year, and there are other advantages.

SLARK.

Perhaps you could get us a cathedral lease.

VICAR.

No doubt I could, Slark, and I am not likely to forget those who were my friends in my days of tribulation.

TWENTY.

Well, say no more about it, sir; I'll wait with pleasure.

SLARK.

And so will I; and I'm sorry I troubled you.

VICAR.

Good-day, my friends. (*Suddenly recollecting.*) Oh, by the way, Mr. Slark, my housekeeper tells me that you were unable to supply any sweetbreads. I know there is sometimes a little difficulty unless they are ordered in plenty of time. Sir Henry's advent was announced to me so suddenly——

SLARK.

Don't say another word, Mr. St. Aubyn; they shall be here in half-an-hour, and anything else you may be pleased to order. Good-day, sir.

TWENTY.

Good-day, sir, and thank you.

VICAR.—(*In grandest manner.*)

Good-day. (*Exeunt Slark and Twentyman.*) Thank God, they're gone! After thirty-five years' experience of duns, I ought to be getting used to them, and imprisonment for debt is happily a thing of the past. Yet somehow or other on these occasions I can never entirely shake off the uncomfortable feeling I used to experience when that barbarous and unchristian practice was in force. (*Enter Mrs. Peel, the housekeeper.*) (*Continues.*) Ah, Mrs. Peel! Has the luncheon arrived yet?

MRS. P.

No, sir.

VICAR.

Dear me! dear me!

MRS. P.

I thought of sending Jane down for it.

VICAR.

Don't do that; it may only irritate Muggles. What do we owe him?

MRS. P.

A matter of fifteen pound.

VICAR.

Nonsense! It can't be that. Come to me again, Mrs. Peel, in a quarter of an hour, if it has not arrived. (*Sound of wheels.*) Gracious Heaven, here is Sir Henry! What on earth is to be done? (*Exit Mrs. Peel to open door.*)

VICAR.

Dear me! dear me!

MRS. F.—(*Without.*)

If he is disengaged——

VICAR.

A woman's voice! thank goodness, it is *not* Sir Henry.

MRS. F.—(*Without.*)

But pray don't trouble him on my account.

VICAR.

On her account! Dear me! Another dun! Is there no end to them?

(*Enter Mrs. Peel and Mrs. Fortescue.*)

MRS. F.

Good morning, Mr. St. Aubyn. (*Vicar bows.*) You don't seem to remember me.

(*Exit Mrs. Peel.*)

VICAR.

Perfectly, madam, perfectly. (*Aside.*) Who *can* it be? Some old debt I've forgotten?

MRS. F.

It's nearly six years since you saw me last.

VICAR.—(*Aside.*)

I understand. She's come to save the Statute of Limitations.

MRS. F.

Being in the neighbourhood I thought I'd look you up, for fear you should forget me altogether.

VICAR.

Forget you, my dear madam! Though circumstances have divided us for so many years I have never forgotten what I owe to you. Believe me it is a debt which I regard almost as one of honour.

MRS. F.

Nonsense, Vicar. Any little service I may have rendered Miriam in years gone by——

VICAR.

Miriam!

MRS. F.

Were given in friendship and with all my heart. You know we were always more like sisters than friends.

VICAR.

Sisters!

MRS. F.

Until my marriage with Mr. Fortescue took me to town, where I am living still.

VICAR.

Bless me, it's Mrs. Fortescue!

MRS. F.

Of course.

VICAR.

Thank Heaven! (*Aside.*) It's not a dun!

MRS. F.

Thank Heaven? What for?

VICAR.

That I am spared to see you once again, looking so well too!

MRS. F.

Yes, I'm pretty fit.

VICAR.

And how is Mr. Fortescue?

MRS. F.

Mr. Fortescue? Bless you, he's been dead two years.

VICAR.

Dear me, you shock me! (*Aside.*) What a merciful release.

MRS. F.—(*Overhearing him.*)

Well, it *was*, rather.

VICAR.

Forgive me for not recognising you; but alas, my eyesight is not what it was. Six years of consumption of the midnight oil——

MRS. F.

Ah, I expect you get it bad down here. I'll send you some of mine. Beautiful whisky, not a trace of oil.

VICAR.

I was alluding to the student's lamp.

MRS. F.

Oh, I misunderstood you.

VICAR.

Years of mental toil are at last beginning to tell on a constitution never too robust. I shall not be sorry when the journey is over. My sole thought is for Miriam. If I could see her happily and comfortably married to some good and worthy man, I should be ready to say with the aged Simeon " Nunc dimittis."

MRS. F.

I don't understand Greek; but if the aged Simeon means that it's an excellent thing for a girl to get married, I quite agree with him. Of course she must find it very dull here.

VICAR.

She has my society.

MRS. F.

Yes, but she wants a little more than that. She

is so pretty, and so clever, that she is really wasting her life down here.

VICAR.

Poor lamb! But what can I do? Nothing, except trust to that Providence which I have never known to fail me.

(*Enter Miriam.*)

MRS. F.

Miriam!

MIRIAM.—(*Surprised.*)

Ethel! (*Embrace.*)

MRS. F.

Then *you've* not forgotten me? My darling, you're prettier than ever.

MIRIAM.

I began to think I should never see you again. Why have you never written to me? You know you promised to write once a month.

MRS. F.

Did I? Then that accounts for it. I am constitutionally incapable of keeping a promise.

MIRIAM.

Well, won't you take your things off? You must stop to luncheon.

(*Mrs. F. takes off her bonnet.*)

VICAR.—(*Aside to Miriam.*)

Has it arrived then?

MIRIAM.

No, papa, not yet.

VICAR.—(*Aside.*)

Dear me! I must send over to Muggles. Providence is failing me for the first time.

MRS. F.

Thank you. I'll just take off my bonnet. I confess, the drive here and the country air have given me an appetite.

VICAR.—(*Aside.*)

Dear me! Dear me!

MRS. F.

But I can't stay.

MIRIAM.—(*Disappointed.*)

Can't stay! (*Vicar tugs at her dress, aside.*)

MRS. F.

No, dear; I'm stopping at the Vivians, ten or twelve miles from here; and I only got permission to pay you a hurried visit on the strict condition that I was back in time for luncheon.

VICAR.—(*Aside.*)

I was too hasty. Providence is very good to me.

Miriam.

Oh, what a pity! I'm so sorry.

Vicar.

Doubtless, you have much to say to one another; and I make it a practice at this hour of the day to devote a brief space of time to meditation.

Mrs. F.

I remember it was always your habit.

Vicar.

It helps me to battle with the trials and difficulties that beset me in this vale of tears. I reap great advantage and assistance from it. I do, indeed.

Mrs. F.

Au revoir then, Mr. St. Aubyn. I hope your meditations will be pleasant.

Vicar.—(*Aside.*)

Now for Muggles! Which will arrive the first? Sir Henry or the luncheon! The excitement is too much for my nerves. Perhaps a little stimulant will steady them.

(*Exit.*)

Mrs. F.

Miriam, my love, does your father take his meditation neat?

MIRIAM.

No, dear, with water—not much water.

MRS. F.

He keeps that for his sermons?

MIRIAM.

He has given up preaching—except at home.

MRS. F.

What does he do then? Meditate?

MIRIAM.

He's generally meditating.

MRS. F.

Humph! that's bad.

MIRIAM.

Except when he is "mixing with his parishioners," to use his own expression.

MRS. F.

Oh, does he mix? That's worse.

MIRIAM.

Or interviewing duns.

MRS. F.

In difficulties again?

MIRIAM.

They're the same difficulties—with six years' interest.

MRS. F.

My poor child! What a life you must lead! I always thought Mr. Fortescue led me rather a life of it, but at least he did not bore me with much of his society. After all, my lot is happier than yours. Poor dear, he took the first opportunity of breaking his neck in the hunting-field, and he has left me very comfortably off.

MIRIAM.

Ethel!

MRS. F.

My love, I was always plain-spoken. I never professed to love my husband; so, you see, I did him no wrong while he was living, nor do I wrong his memory now he is dead.

MIRIAM.

I wonder you don't marry again; and this time, someone that you really care for.

MRS. F.

Not I. I have something better in view than a mere love match. Do you happen to know Sir Henry Craven? I believe he has property in the neighbourhood.

MIRIAM.

Sir Henry Craven? We expect him this morning.

MRS. F.

What a remarkable coincidence! It is Sir Henry whom I have in view.

MIRIAM.

Then, Ethel, I'm afraid I am your rival.

MRS. F.

You! I retire from the contest. I will not compete with you for the Craven Stakes! My love, you may consider me scratched.

MIRIAM.

I have only seen him twice, but he tells papa that he shall have no peace of mind until I promise to marry him. Of course, papa wants to bring this about. Sir Henry has immense interest and would be certain to get him some preferment.

MRS. F.

I cannot say your father is wrong. Think of your position—the wife of an ambassador—Good heavens! It would be madness to refuse.

MIRIAM.

But I couldn't bear to be tied to a man I didn't love. And I could never love Sir Henry.

MRS. F.

You don't know what you can do till you try. I did wonders in the way of loving Mr. Fortescue; and, my dear child—I don't want to say anything cruel—but if a woman could love Mr. Fortescue, she could love anybody.

(*Sound of wheels. Re-enter Vicar, who takes Miriam aside excitedly.*)

VICAR.

Sir Henry has arrived before the luncheon.

MIRIAM.

Hasn't it come yet?

VICAR.

Its advent is delayed, but my faith is unabated. Providence, that feedeth the sparrows, will not desert me in my hour of need.

(*Enter Sir Henry Craven, shown in by Mrs. Peel, followed by Valet, who exits with Mrs. Peel.*)

SIR H.

I'm very glad to see you again, St. Aubyn. Ah, Miss St. Aubyn, how are you? I need hardly ask. Mrs. Fortescue! This is an unexpected pleasure.

MRS. F.

I am flattered that you should think so, Sir Henry.

VICAR.—(*Aside.*)

Wants to hook him herself. I wish she'd go. Widows are so very dangerous.

SIR H.—(*Looking out of window.*)

A very pretty place, St. Aubyn, but rather dull, I should imagine, in winter.

VICAR.

"O! fortunatos nimium, sua si bona norint, Agricolas!" Ha! ha! (*Aside.*) A Dean should always be a learned man. He shall see I have kept up my classics.

SIR H.—(*Puzzled.*)

Exactly so. What I have always felt myself. Poor Peel used to say that every man should know his Horace by heart; but I never really had the time.

VICAR.—(*Aside.*)

I quoted Virgil; but I had better not correct Sir Henry.

SIR H.

Well, Miss St. Aubyn, how do you like Devonshire? For myself I think it is one of the loveliest counties. I hope, to-morrow, that you will let me see a little of the neighbourhood.

VICAR.

I am sure Miriam will be delighted to act as your guide.

MIRIAM.

I shall be pleased to do anything in my power; but my father knows more about it than I do.

SIR H.

I am sure your father must be too busied with his parochial work to spare many moments for archæology.

VICAR.

I am afraid that is so, although at the same time archæology in all its branches has always been my favourite pursuit.

SIR H.

Then it is understood that Miss St. Aubyn will act as my guide.

MRS. F.

No wonder you love Devonshire, Sir Henry. Who could help loving it? It almost reminds me of Nice and Mentone.

VICAR.—(*Aside.*)

This widow will spoil everything!
(*Takes Mrs. F. aside.*)

SIR H.

The climate seems identical. Of course you have seen the Mediterranean, Miss St. Aubyn?

MIRIAM.

No, indeed. I have scarcely been away from here.

SIR H.

Dear me, what a pity! You ought, at least, to have been to London for the season, and to have been presented, and to have gone to Ascot and Cowes. It is dreadful to think of your having been buried here.

MIRIAM.

My father is not to blame that I have not seen the places you mention. His income is not a large one, and he could not afford the extravagances you refer to.

VICAR.

My dear Craven, you are quite right. This place is lonely, desolate, and remote. Miriam has no companions of her own age; nor has she those innocent enjoyments which it is the chief sorrow of my life that I am unable to provide for her.

MRS. F.—(*Aside.*)

The old gentleman is riding to win. Anything more unblushing I never saw.

Sir H.

All this must be changed. Your father, Miss St. Aubyn, has hidden himself too much. He should without delay resume his fitting position in the world—a position distinctly due to his birth, his connections, and his great natural gifts.

Vicar.

Oh, Sir Henry, you exaggerate!

Sir H.

Not the least in the world.

Mrs. F.—(*Aside.*)

They call women liars, but for downright unblushing mendacity commend me to this old diplomatist.

Sir H.

Now, St. Aubyn, I come to the important point. The Deanery of Southwick is vacant.

Vicar.

Dear me! Dear me! Is the Dean —— ?

Sir H.

Dr. Proby died last night.

Vicar.

Poor Proby! Poor, poor Proby!

Sir H.

My personal influence with the Premier, to say nothing of His Grace the Archbishop, will make the matter a foregone conclusion. What do you think of the matter, Miss St. Aubyn? Shouldn't you like to get away from here?

Vicar.

Poor, poor Proby!

Miriam.

I should like to get away—at least I think so—though I love the poor people, and I am afraid they would miss me very much. But in anything that is for papa's advantage I should rejoice.

Sir H.

Now, St. Aubyn, one word with you, as I must send a telegram. Let us come to your study.

Mrs. F.

Don't let us disturb you. Miriam and I will go into the garden. We have not seen each other for so long, and have millions of things to talk about. Come along, Miriam. (*Aside.*) What a dear old man.

Miriam.

I hate him!

Mrs. F.

My love, he's perfectly charming, and his smile does the greatest credit to his dentist.

(*Exeunt Mrs. F. and Miriam.*)

Vicar.

Sir Henry, how shall I ever thank you?

Sir H.

Don't talk of thanks between friends such as we are; and I trust that ere long we may have a closer connection. St. Aubyn, I am very much struck with your daughter. She would be an ornament to any man's dinner table. I am perhaps a little too old for her.

Vicar.—(*Deprecatingly.*)

Oh, no!

Sir H.

Yes, I am not as young as I could wish. But what of that?

Vicar.

What, indeed? Sir Henry, you overwhelm me with your splendid proposals. I look upon my daughter as one of the most fortunate girls in the world. (*Aside.*) He has said nothing about the settlements, but I need have no fear.

Sir H.

Very well, St. Aubyn, then it is understood. Perhaps you will speak to your daughter.

Vicar.

It shall be as you wish. How can I thank you, my dear Craven? To some men their reward comes late in life and to others early. I have still some few years left, in which, to the best of my humble abilities, to serve my Queen, my Church, and my country. What more could a man desire? (*Smiles sweetly, but is evidently suffering from suppressed excitement.*)

Sir H.—(*Good-naturedly.*)

You have still many years before you, my dear St. Aubyn, and it is out of our Deans that Ministers select our Bishops. You have had your foot on the first step of the ladder far too long, but Miriam and I will yet see you at its summit.

Vicar.

All things are ordered wisely and divinely.

Sir H.—(*Aside.*)

I wonder he did not say "Propria quae maribus," or "Mars, Bacchus, Apollo virorum," it would have been equally classical and equally appropriate.
(*Re-enter Miriam and Mrs. Fortescue.*)

MIRIAM.

Papa, luncheon is ready.

VICAR.—(*Aside.*)

My prayer is heard! I was beginning to fear that Muggles' heart had been hardened like that of Pharaoh of old.

SIR H.

Miss St. Aubyn, I have good news for you. In a few hours your father will be Dean of Southwick. I tell you what it is, St. Aubyn, I ought to return to town at once and clinch the matter. When does the afternoon train leave?

VICAR.

A few minutes after three.

SIR H.—(*Looking at watch.*)

I have just time to catch it. Miss St. Aubyn, your father has a communication to make to you. If Mrs. Fortescue will give me a mouthful of lunch I shall be grateful.

MRS. F.

Certainly, Sir Henry, you must be famished after your journey.

(*Exeunt Mrs. F. and Sir H.*)

VICAR.

I wonder if it is safe to leave them together? (*Looking off.*)

MIRIAM.

Well, papa, please go on and let us get it over.

VICAR.

I suppose, Miriam, that you have some idea of the nature of the important communication which I have to make to you?

MIRIAM.

Oh, yes, Mrs. Peel tells me that you have been talking about it all over the village. Everyone knows that the money you owe Mr. Slark, and Mr. Twentyman, and Mr. Muggles can wait, and that they are to be paid when you have married me to Sir Henry Craven, and got your Deanery.

VICAR.

My dear Miriam!

MIRIAM.

Oh, I understand it, papa. The question is whether I am to be made miserable for life in order to serve your purposes.

VICAR.

My dear child, I confess I am deeply grieved

and wounded. I have been, Miriam, a loving and tender parent to you.

MIRIAM.

I have always been a dutiful daughter, and have never once complained of the joyless life I have been compelled to lead. I am ready to continue that life and to put up with even greater discomfort, but I see no reason why I should be given to this old man, who, if he had a spark of feeling in his nature, would not demand such a sacrifice.

VICAR.

You wrong Sir Henry. Sir Henry loves you with all the courtly devotion of a man of culture and refinement. I am getting old, Miriam. I may be summoned at any moment. (*Affects a look of resignation to the decrees of Providence.*) I promised your dearest mother that I would watch over you.

MIRIAM.

Oh, papa, pray leave my mother out of the question. If she had been here, you would never have dared to attempt to make a bargain over me, just as if you were buying and selling in market.

VICAR.

Miriam, if you will be good enough to abstain from being rude and to listen to me, we shall probably come to a wiser and proper conclusion.

MIRIAM.

It is useless discussing this subject any further. I shall not marry Sir Henry.

VICAR.

Great Heaven! Grant me patience! This man holds one of the first positions in diplomacy. He is immensely rich, and will probably settle a hundred thousand pounds on you. And prospects like these you propose to throw to the winds!

MIRIAM.

Please say no more. You have for years done all in your power to alienate my affections from you, and every word you utter widens the gulf between us.

VICAR.

You seem strangely unmindful of the Divine command, "Honour thy father." But I will leave you to search your heart. (*Aside.*) And I feel that I really require something to sustain me. (*Aloud.*) Miriam, if anything could reconcile me

to your poor mother's loss, it is the thought that she has at least been spared this painful spectacle.
(*Exit Vicar.*)

MIRIAM.

What shall I do? After all, anything is better than remaining in this horrid place. But why should I marry Sir Henry that my father may be made a Dean? Even Jephthah did not propose to sell his daughter for a daily mess of pottage. I will *not* marry Sir Henry. Suppose, when it was too late, I were to meet a man I really could love, and who loved me, young, handsome, brave and true, not an old mummy with stays and paint, but a noble, generous, honest man. The thought is too awful. I will *not* accept Sir Henry.
(*Re-enter Mrs. Fortescue.*)

MRS. F.

My dear child, your father has just told me what has happened. Sir Henry has proposed for you.

MIRIAM.

Yes, and I have told papa that I will not hear of it.

MRS. F.

You are making a great mistake, Miriam; life

is far too short to warrant any of us in throwing away so splendid an opportunity.

MIRIAM.

I cannot bear Sir Henry—in my eyes he is odious.

MRS. F.

Just how I felt towards Mr. Fortescue. But lor! I soon got used to him. My dear, when you've been married a year or two you don't take any notice of your husband. You have to think even whether he's dark or fair.

MIRIAM.

When I marry I mean to marry a man that I can love, not an old fossil that might be my grandfather.

MRS. F.

Rubbish, my dear child. Boys are like green apples. Give me a middle-aged or even an elderly man, a ripe, round, ribston pippin.

MIRIAM.

Why should I sacrifice myself? My father only urges it for his own purposes.

MRS. F.

Your father's interests happen to be identical

with your own. So much the better. If he gets his deanery, he will be able to support himself without sponging upon you.

MIRIAM.

I only wish Sir Henry had fallen in love with someone else.

MRS. F.

You had better make hay while the sun shines, or that is precisely what he will be doing.

MIRIAM.

Don't imagine that I want to stay on here and continue this wretched life that I have been leading for years. If I met a man that I could love and respect, I should be glad to escape from my present misery.

MRS. F.

Put away dreams, my child. The world is real, prosaic, sordid if you like, but one must take it as one finds it; and the only thing to be done is to make yourself as comfortable as you can. If you refuse Sir Henry, your father is ruined, and you will go to the wall with him. Without this marriage your future is hopeless.

MIRIAM.

You think it is my duty.

MRS. F.

I am sure of it.

(*Re-enter Sir Henry and Vicar, wiping his mouth.*)

SIR H.

My dear Miss St. Aubyn, your father tells me that he has communicated my proposals to you. May I trust that they are not distasteful to you? I await your decision with an anxiety I have never before experienced.

VICAR.—(*Aside.*)

And so do I, Heaven knows!

MIRIAM.

My father says that you wish me to marry you, Sir Henry; I will do so.

SIR H.—(*With enthusiasm.*)

My dear Miriam, you have made me the happiest man in England. You shall never repent your choice. (*Kisses her hand—Miriam recoils.*)

VICAR.

Heaven bless you, my dear child. Poor Proby!
(*Re-enter Valet.*)

VALET.

The fly is at the door, Sir Henry. There is only just time to catch the express.
(*Exit Valet.*)

Sir H.

Very well, then I must tear myself away. I shall be back, St. Aubyn, in forty-eight hours, and you will be Dean of Southwick. Good-bye, Mrs. Fortescue. Good-bye, Miriam; you have made me the proudest man in England. (*Kisses Miriam's hand, shakes hands with the Vicar, and Exit.*)

Mrs. F.

All's well that ends well, and nothing could have ended better. My dear Miriam, you'll be the envy of every unmarried girl in town.

Vicar.

I am humbly thankful that Providence, in its infinite bounty, has given my beloved daughter to so worthy a husband. (*Sits.*)

Miriam.

No, papa, let there be no mistake. Heaven has nothing to do with it. I am not given, but *sold*.

Vicar.

Poor Proby! (*With eyes upturned, taking no notice of Miriam.*)

End of Act I.

ACT II.

SCENE.—DRAWING ROOM IN ST. JAMES'S SQUARE.

(*Enter Prince Balanikoff, shown in by Elise, Lady Craven's maid.*)

PRINCE.

Well, Mdlle. Elise, what news have you for me to-day?

ELISE.

Not a great deal, Monsieur le Prince. Things are going on much in the same way. My Lady and Sir Henry quarrel always.

PRINCE.

And Mr. Sabine?

ELISE.

Is here all the days.

PRINCE.

Ah! Let me know if anything of importance occurs. You have not lost the address?

ELISE.

No, Monsieur le Prince.

PRINCE.

Here is something to buy you some more ribbons. (*Gives Elise a £5 note.*) And now, let your mistress know that I am here.

ELISE.

Merci, Monsieur le Prince! Monsieur le Prince shall hear everything.

(*Exit Elise with the Prince's card.*)

PRINCE.

These English are wonderful! Marvellous! Here is this old fossil, Sir Henry, married, by some extraordinary freak of fortune, to a young and charming wife, spending his time and his money on a painted harridan that no man of position dare be seen with— a creature as ugly as Satan and as stupid as your feet. If Lady Craven knew what was going on she might revenge herself, if only to show her independence. Bah! She must find out one day, and then *nous autres* will have our chance. *Tout vient à point à qui sait attendre.*

(*Enter Mrs. Fortescue.*)

MRS. F.

How do you do, Prince?

PRINCE.

How is my charming friend, Mrs. Fortescue?

MRS. F.

Rather tired. I have been sitting up with Lady Craven, who was very ill last night. I am afraid she is not well enough to receive you, Prince.

PRINCE.

Lady Craven seems anything but strong. She always appears to me as if she had something on her mind. I hope her husband's escapades have not come to her ears. Even if they have, I cannot see why they should distress her.

MRS. F.—(*Aside.*)

What's this about escapades?

PRINCE.

A charming and adorable divinity like Lady Craven can have no possible occasion to be jealous.

MRS. F.

Of course not, Prince, of course. But at the same time, women are so sensitive, that is, *some* women.

PRINCE.

I hope she is not taking it to heart.

MRS. F.

Hush, Prince! (*Aside.*) What does he mean?

I'm on the verge of some discovery. (*Aloud.*) Such things are best not talked about.

PRINCE.

In public—but you are a woman of the world.

MRS. F.

I never listen to scandal. Please to say no more.

PRINCE.

I will obey you; not another word shall pass my lips.

MRS. F.—(*Aside.*)

Oh, yes, there shall. (*Aloud.*) I quite agree with you, that Lady Craven has no occasion to be jealous of so very unworthy a rival.

PRINCE.

I'm told she was a housemaid originally.

MRS. F.

Don't speak of it. (*Aside.*) An escapade with a housemaid, oh!

PRINCE.

It is extraordinary, but *chacun à son gout.*

MRS. F.

Prince, let us change the subject. It is a painful one. I do not wish to hear another word about— really I forget the creature's name.

PRINCE.

Mrs. Montressor.

MRS. F.

Yes, Mrs. Montressor. (*Aside.*) An intrigue with a Mrs. Montressor!

PRINCE.

Mrs. Fortescue, I make you my compliments. You seem to be exempt from all the foibles of your sex—even from curiosity.

MRS. F.

How can I possibly be curious upon a subject of which, alas, I hear only too much, which will soon be the common talk of every Club in London?

PRINCE.

It is already the talk of the Clubs.

MRS. F.—(*Aside.*)

Oh! it's the talk of the Clubs!

PRINCE.

Poor Lady Craven has the sympathy of everyone, and mine especially.

MRS. F.—(*Severely.*)

Prince, not another word. (*Aside.*) Here's a

discovery! (*Goes up.*) I will tell Lady Craven you are here.
(*Exit.*)

PRINCE.—(*Bows, aside.*)

What a waste of time is diplomacy! If I had said to that woman, I am dying to tell you that Sir Henry is false to his wife, and she had said to me I am dying to hear all about it, what trouble we should have saved one another!
(*Re-enter Mrs. Fortescue.*)

MRS. F.

Lady Craven is lying down, and is absolutely unable to move her head from the pillow.
(*Enter Miriam at opposite door.*)

PRINCE.

Indeed. Then, I must congratulate her on the rapidity of her recovery.

MIRIAM.

From what, Prince?

PRINCE.

From your illness.

MIRIAM.—(*Not observing Mrs. Fortescue's frantic signals.*)

Thank you very much, but I was never better in my life.

PRINCE.

I am charmed to hear it, and must apologise to Mrs. Fortescue for having misunderstood her. I am not yet quite master of your English language.

MRS. F.

Pray don't apologise. I was always a *femme incomprise*. (*Turns off.*)

MIRIAM.

You are out early this morning. Sir Henry is still in his study. I'm sure he will be delighted to see you.

PRINCE.—(*Aside to her passionately.*)

I did not come to see Sir Henry. I came to see *you*. Will you not give me a minute—a moment? You are never alone.

MIRIAM.—(*Aloud.*)

My time is yours, Prince. Anything you have to say, you can say before Mrs. Fortescue. She is discretion itself.

PRINCE.—(*Aloud—with assumed indifference.*)

Pardon. It is not anything. I merely called to ask after your health.

MIRIAM.

It is everything I could desire. (*Smiling.*)

PRINCE.—(*Aside to her.*)

Ah! You are cruel!

MIRIAM.

Won't you sit down? I expect Sir Henry every moment.

PRINCE.

You are very kind; but I cannot give myself the pleasure of remaining.

MIRIAM.

I think I hear him.

PRINCE.

I have an appointment. Will you convey to him my compliments? (*Mrs. Fortescue rings.*) Adieu!
(*Miriam gives him her hand, which he is about to raise to his lips, when she withdraws it.*)
(*Re-enter Elise.*)

MIRIAM.

Elise, the door.

PRINCE.

Good morning, Mrs. Fortescue.

MRS. F.

Ta, ta!
(*Exit Prince, with a glance at Miriam and Elise.*)

MIRIAM.

Thank goodness. I thought he was never going.

MRS. F.

I am sure the poor man did not stay long. I cannot understand your snubbing him.

MIRIAM.

His admiration is utterly distasteful to me. Why should I encourage him?

MRS. F.

One never knows what may happen, and it is always advisable to have more than one string to your bow.

MIRIAM.

More than one string?

MRS. F.

Strings break and want replacing.

MIRIAM.

You forget that I am married.

MRS. F.

That's just what I was remembering. After marriage the tension is greater than before, and a prudent wife provides against emergencies.

MIRIAM.

Ethel, what *do* you mean?

MRS. F.

What I say. Also, what I *don't* say.

MIRIAM.

How can you talk in that way! I am married, and there is an end of it.

MRS. F.

In Devonshire; but in London, marriage is only the beginning of it.

MIRIAM.

That is not my idea of marriage. Ah me, how idly one dreams, and how rude is the awaking.

MRS. F.

Then you *have* awakened?

MIRIAM.

Yes; I understand now why Sir Henry has married me. I am part and parcel of the furniture of his house. He bought me as he might have bought a statue to stand in a corner, or a picture to hang on the wall.

MRS. F.

And you are willing to accept that position? Why, my dear, he doesn't even hang you on the line.

MIRIAM.

Have I not already accepted it? Nobody compelled me to marry Sir Henry. I knew quite well what I was about, and in spite of his unkindness I intend to do my duty.

MRS. F.

I have not advised you to do otherwise. All I suggested was, that in the event of Sir Henry and yourself becoming estranged, you would find an influential friend in Prince Balanikoff.

MIRIAM.

I want no friend of that description.

MRS. F.

Princes are not to be despised.

MIRIAM.

I should no more think of looking for a friend in Prince Balanikoff than I should expect guidance and assistance from the Dean.

MRS. F.

Very well, my dear, I can appreciate your standpoint, though I must admit that it is far too high a one for me. I was never a climber, moral or physical. But I must say the least you can do is to be consistent, and when Mr. Sabine calls say you are not at home.

MIRIAM.

He has gone to Paris and is not likely to be back for some little time.

MRS. F.

You seem quite *au courant* with his movements.

MIRIAM.

I don't think you like Mr. Sabine.

MRS. F.

On the contrary I like him immensely.

MIRIAM.

He is one of the few men I have met whom it is impossible not to admire. He is so frank and manly, so honest and sincere, the best and truest friend I have ever known.

MRS. F.—(*Aside.*)

That's one for me.

(*Enter Sir Henry Craven.*)

SIR H.

Good morning, Miriam; good morning, Mrs. Fortescue. I am sorry that I shall be compelled to leave town for a few days. Most delicate and important negotiations in connection with my mission to Constantinople render this necessary.

MIRIAM.—(*Going to him.*)

I should like to be behind the scenes in all these great state secrets. I am certain that I have a natural taste for diplomacy, as some people have a taste for music, and with a little tuition——.

SIR H.—(*Interrupting her.*)

Diplomacy is no doubt a natural gift, as is a correct ear for music, and so far as my experience has enabled me to judge it is one of those gifts which are hereditary.

MRS. F.—(*Aside.*)

That's one for *her*. I'll give *him two* directly.

SIR H.

Diplomacy, my dear Miriam, is like the habit of setting to the scent of game in the pointer.

MRS. F.—(*Aside.*)

Two lovely black ones!

SIR H.

You cannot teach a Newfoundland or a greyhound to set to game.

MIRIAM.—(*Sadly.*)

I think I understand you.

MRS. F.—(*Aside.*)

It's more than he does himself. (*Aloud.*) Ah! Sir Henry, you have such a marvellous way of putting things (*Sir H. bows.*) (*Aside.*) —wrong.

SIR H.

Well, I am, through the perversity of fate, sent to Constantinople to listen to lies for my country's good, and tell, if possible, bigger lies in the same sacred cause.

MIRIAM.

Not actual lies, I hope.

SIR H.

Yes, Miriam, I am afraid so. The telling of lies is the function of us men at present. Since the original fall it has ceased to be the business of a lady.

MRS. F.

Now it's her recreation.

SIR H.

Ha! ha! ha! that's what I meant, of course.

MRS. F.—(*Aside.*)

Of course it wasn't.

MIRIAM.

Are you leaving then, to-day, Sir Henry?

SIR H.

Yes, I have to see the Prime Minister.

MIRIAM.

You said nothing about it before.

SIR H.

Didn't I? Then I must have forgotten. (*Re-enter Elise with card.*) Gracious me! Say that I am out! (*Passes card to Miriam.*)

MIRIAM.

We are *both* out. (*Passes card to Mrs. F.*)

MRS. F.

We are *all* out.

(*Enter Dean, exit Elise.*)

SIR H.—(*Aside.*)

Too late!

DEAN.

My dear Sir Henry, how fortunate I am to find you at home.

SIR H.

Good morning.

DEAN.

My dearest Miriam, God bless you! How well you are looking. You amply repay many years of toil and anxiety and self-denial.

MIRIAM.

What has brought you to town, papa?

DEAN.

I will not trouble you with the reasons of my advent. Suffice it to say that they were not altogether unconnected with the sacred cause of charity.

MRS. F.—(*Aside.*)

A charity that begins at home, I'll be bound.

DEAN.

I really had no time to apprise you of my arrival, and, indeed, I thought I would give myself the pleasure of taking you by surprise.

MRS. F.—(*Aside to Miriam.*)

Crafty old fox!

MIRIAM.—(*Aside to Mrs. F.*)

He knew that Sir Henry would put him off.

SIR H.

I am sure, Dean, we are delighted to see you.

DEAN.

A thousand thanks, Sir Henry, for the Madeira that you were kind enough to send me. The Bishop told me had never tasted such a wine. Indeed, his Lordship liked it so well that he has almost finished the case. Hem!

Sir H.

I will send you some more.

Dean.

I wouldn't give you the trouble for the world. You have so much to think of. (*Sits.*) Things seem to be in a very unsettled state. The horizon appears very cloudy, and seems to presage an impending storm.

Mrs. F.

Can I lend you an umbrella?

Dean.

I was referring to the political outlook. A wave of anarchy is passing over us. I have myself no sympathy with the movement. It is not for man to rebel when Providence showers its bounties in his lap; and to resign them to the common weal, to my mind, savours of ingratitude.

Sir H.

I've no intention of resigning anything; I mean in future to button up my pockets.

Dean.

Hem! of course, I would not dam the stream of charity, which blesseth him that giveth even more than him that receiveth. And that reminds me; I am most anxious to ask your advice.

SIR H.

What is it?

DEAN.

It is in relation to a matter partaking somewhat of a financial nature.

MIRIAM.—(*Aside.*)

I might have guessed this was coming.

DEAN.

The fact is, the expenses of moving into the Deanery have been enormous, and I have been obliged in consequence to heavily overdraw my account at the County Bank. Now, at the County Bank they are extremely courteous, but, at the same time, extremely old-fashioned.

SIR H.

In what way can I help you?

MIRIAM.

I am sorry, papa, that you should have troubled Sir Henry.

DEAN.

Figures were always my abhorrence. In financial matters I am almost as a babe and suckling.

MRS. F.—(*Rising.*)

Pray let me go if you have any private matters to discuss. I would not dam the stream of charity for the world; and I am afraid I shall, if I stop here.

DEAN.

Sir Henry, I think I could make my meaning more clear if you would grant me the favour of a private interview, which need not necessarily be of prolonged duration.

SIR H.

Certainly. Come into the library; there is no one there.

DEAN.—(*Aside.*)

I hate these cold plunges. But it is well to take them boldly, and not to linger on the brink. (*Aloud to Miriam.*) I will not keep your husband long from you, my darling.

(*Exeunt Sir Henry and the Dean.*)

MRS. F,

Your father is a phenomenon. I can myself on occasion turn on a little hypocrisy, but when your father is by I feel myself at the feet of Gamaliel.

MIRIAM.

I am indignant that he should lay himself under

these obligations to Sir Henry. If he wanted money, he should have written to me, and I would have done the best I could for him.

Mrs. F.

Never mind Sir Henry. He is quite capable of taking care of himself. Get all you can out of him and lose no time. You may be sure if *you* don't, somebody else *will*.

Miriam.

What do you mean?

Mrs. F.

I only made a general observation.

Miriam.

You can't deceive me, Ethel. You know my wretched life, and you are sorry for me; I can often see it in your face. Dear Ethel, you are keeping something back. You can't make things much worse; I fear you can never make them better, but tell me the truth.

Mrs. F.

All I meant was it is better that you and your father should have Sir Henry's money than that it should go out of the family.

MIRIAM.

Out of the family!

MRS. F.

Don't look at me with those great, innocent eyes. Can't you take a hint? You are one of those ultra-innocent persons to whom it is impossible to convey an idea without using language unbecoming a respectable widow—otherwise they don't understand you.

MIRIAM.

What *are* you driving at?

MRS. F.

Well, my dear Miriam, you *must* know that your husband is not as innocent as *you* are—that he is what is called " a man of the world."

MIRIAM.

Of course; though I confess I could never quite understand what " a man of the world " is.

MRS. F.

There I can quite sympathise with you. I've been trying to make it out all my life; and I have come to the conclusion that " a man of the world " is a man who knows better, and does worse.

MIRIAM.

I am as wise as ever.

MRS. F.

Well, if you *will* have it in black and white, a man whose taste is so catholic, whose heart is so cosmopolitan, that it embraces more women than his wife.

MIRIAM.

Ethel!

MRS. F.

The murder's out!

MIRIAM.

You accuse Sir Henry.

MRS. F.

Yes, I accuse Sir Henry!

MIRIAM.

Of being unfaithful?

MRS. F.

Yes, of being unfaithful.

MIRIAM.

With whom?

MRS. F.

A Mrs. Montressor.

MIRIAM.

What proof have you?

Mrs. F.

Not the least little bit in the world.

MIRIAM.

I don't believe a word of it. My husband has his faults. He is neglectful and sometimes cruel, but he would never be so base as this! I don't believe it, and I will not listen to such scandal.

MRS. F.

My dear, it's a deceitful world, and you're quite right not to believe *anything*; but *listen* to *everything*. After all, nothing is more probable. Men are all alike! Mr. Fortescue was not a saint. I intercepted a letter, my dear, that opened my eyes, at once communicated with the lady's husband, and Mr. Fortescue couldn't open his eyes for a fortnight.

MIRIAM.

I shall not doubt *my* husband, unless I have positive proof.

(*Enter Elise.*)

ELISE.

Mr. Sabine is here, my lady.

Miriam.—(*Starting.*)

Mr. Sabine!

Mrs. F.

Lady Craven is lying down and——

Miriam.—(*Aside to Mrs. F.*)

Ethel!

(*Elise watches her mistress like a cat.*)

(*To Elise.*) Tell Mr. Sabine I will see him.
(*Exit Elise.*)

Mrs. F.

I *thought* you'd see him!

Miriam.

You are quite mistaken in my motives. But I own that I like to see Mr. Sabine. His visits always seem to cheer me up.
(*Enter Sabine.*)

Miriam.

Mr. Sabine! (*General greeting.*) I thought you were in Paris!

Mr. S.

I returned this morning.

Mrs. F.—(*Aside.*)

He hasn't lost much time. (*Aloud.*) One's never sure of you. One day you're in London, and the next in the Rocky Mountains.

MR. S.

Well, I'm not the only traveller. I understand, Lady Craven, that you will soon be going to Constantinople?

MIRIAM.

Yes, I suppose so; but as yet nothing is settled. Do you think I shall like it?

MR. S.

I think you'll loathe it.

MRS. F.

What are the Turkish ladies like?

MR. S.

They are far more stupid and uninteresting than the young ladies from a select academy in the suburbs, which receives the daughters of commercial gentlemen upon reciprocal terms.

MIRIAM.

What do they do all day?

MR. S.

Eat lollipops. They devour sugar-plums and cake by the hundredweight, smoke cigarettes, and when they can get it, drink brandy and soda.

MRS. F.

I shouldn't mind that at all.

MIRIAM.

From what you tell me, I shouldn't think that they were very lively society.

MRS. F.

Excuse me, Miriam. I have a letter to write and I'm afraid that I shall miss the post.

MIRIAM.

Certainly, dear. (*Mr. S. bows.*)

MRS. F.

Good morning. (*Aside.*) Two's company — three's a nuisance. He hasn't called to talk about Turks.
(*Exit.*)

MR. S.

Then you really contemplate leaving England?

MIRIAM.

Of course I must accompany my husband.

MR. S.

I am more sorry than I can say.

MIRIAM.

Sorry, Mr. Sabine!

MR. S.

Sometimes I think that this world is really very badly arranged. It might have been so very interesting, and it *is* such a bore. Fate seems to take a perverse delight in casting one's lot among people to whom one is absolutely indifferent, and in separating one from those in whose company one takes pleasure.

MIRIAM.

Unfortunately we can't alter it. We must take it as we find it.

MR. S.

But sometimes we can alter it. It is the lazy habit of taking things as we find them that is responsible for the mischief.

MIRIAM.

What can we do?

MR. S.

What we like. If we did a great deal more as we liked, and a great deal less as we were told, the world would be very much happier.

MIRIAM.

But would it be better?

MR. S.

Certainly. It is quite a mistake to suppose that men wish to do evil. Moralists tells us we are never so happy as when we are good. That is a truism:

the truth is we are never so good as when we are happy.

MIRIAM.

Yours is a pleasant creed.

MR. S.

Why should it not be? I can never understand why duty should always be disagreeable; but I believe that the natural instincts of a sound man or woman are a much safer guide than any system of moral philosophy.

MIRIAM.

To what are you alluding?

MR. S.

To your exile at Constantinople. Do you really wish to leave town?

MIRIAM.

I dread the thought of it. I am not often happy in London, but I am *never* happy out of it.

MR. S.

Then why leave it?

MIRIAM.

A wife must obey her husband.

MR. S.

Does Sir Henry insist upon your going?

MIRIAM.

He has not so much as mentioned it; but, of course, he will expect me to accompany him.

MR. S.

I have no right to say any more. I can only wish you a very pleasant journey; and *that* I happen to know you will have. Sir Henry has made every arrangement for your comfort. He is certainly a model husband.

MIRIAM.

Sir Henry has told you of his arrangements?

MR. S.

No. I have discovered them by accident. The manager of the Chemin de Fer de Lyon et Méditerranée, who is an old acquaintance of mine, happened to mention to me two or three days ago, when I was in Paris, that he had just received instructions as to your journey. He asked me if I knew Sir Henry, and I told him that I did slightly.

MIRIAM.

Did he tell you anything else?

MR. S.

Yes; that Sir Henry feared it would fatigue you to accompany him direct, and so had arranged for you to travel alone, taking the journey by easy stages. You are to be treated like a Princess. He has even arranged that you are to travel incognita.

MIRIAM.

Incognita!

MR. S.

Under the name of Mrs. Montressor.

MIRIAM.

Indeed!

MR. S.

What a curious thing that he should not have mentioned the matter to you. Perhaps he meant to give you a pleasant surprise. If so, I've anticipated him.

MIRIAM.

No; I don't think you have.

MR. S.

Otherwise I can't understand it.

MIRIAM.

I understand it—perfectly.

(*Re-enter Mrs. Fortescue.*)

MRS. F.

I caught the post after all. Still on the subject of the Turks?

(*Mr. Sabine goes up to meet Sir Henry, who re-enters on the other side.*)

(*Re-enter Dean on same side as Sir Henry, radiant, slipping a cheque into his pocket-book.*)

DEAN.—(*Returning his pocket-book to his breast-pocket.*)

How full of thankfulness we ought to be to a bountiful Providence.

MRS. F.

We ought, indeed, Mr. St. Aubyn; but I can never understand why people who trust so much to Providence in Heaven should trust so little to it on earth.

SIR H.

I am very pleased to see you, Mr. Sabine. I heard you were in Paris.

MR. S.

So I was. I came back this morning just in time to say good-bye to you and Lady Craven. I suppose you will be off to Constantinople almost immediately.

SIR H.

Yes, in a very few days now; but your good-bye will be for me alone.

MR. S.

Alone!

SIR H.

Lady Craven will not accompany me

MR. S.—(*Astounded.*)

Your wife is not going with you?

SIR H.

She is not very strong, and I am sure the climate would not suit her.

MR. S.—(*Aside.*)

Great Heaven! what have I done? (*Stands looking at Miriam—their eyes meet.*)

SIR H.—(*To Mr. S.*)

Then, again, Lady Craven has no natural genius for diplomacy. (*To Miriam, pleasantly and courteously.*) I can promise you, my dear, that I shall never trouble you by asking you to take any serious part in my labours. No, my dear Miriam, I never for one moment dreamt of taking you. Mr. Sabine, I wish you good morning. Can I give you a lift in my brougham?

MR. S.

Thank you, Sir Henry, I will come with you.

SIR H.

I hope you will sometimes call. My wife and Mrs. Fortescue will be in town till the end of the season. Good-bye, Dean.
(*Exit.*)

MR. S.

Lady Craven, can you ever forgive me?

MIRIAM.

Forgive you? Yes. I thank you. Now good-bye. (*Offers hand.*)

MR. S.—(*Taking it.*)

May I call?

MIRIAM.

No.
(*Exit Mr. S.*)

(*Miriam bursts into tears.*)

DEAN.

My sweetest child! Tell me what is your trouble?

MRS. F.—(*Putting her arm round Miriam.*)

Miriam is not very well; I do not think that I would bother her.

MIRIAM.

See what you have done! See what all your planning and scheming have come to.

DEAN.

What is the matter, child?

MIRIAM.

I am the most wretched woman in the world.

DEAN.

Wretched! You, the honoured wife of a good husband; the daughter of a dignitary of the Church. It is positively wicked to be wretched. Be worthy of your early training. Be worthy, above all, of the good and distinguished man who has given you his name. What says the Psalmist? "A good wife——"

MIRIAM.

Silence, father! I am the miserable wife of a heartless and wicked man.

DEAN.

What on earth can you mean?

MRS. F.

Don't worry her! Can you not see that your daughter is suffering?

MIRIAM.—(*To Dean.*)

After all, you are my father, and I will tell you. Not content with utterly neglecting me, not content with making me submit to cold, heartless, and cruel treatment, Sir Henry has ended by refusing to take me with him to Constantinople—and has supplied my place.

MRS. F.

Now, Mr. Dean, what have you to say?

DEAN.

Simply that I don't believe it. Some evil-minded person, with reasons of his own—possibly *her* own—has misinformed you.

MIRIAM.

I am certain it is true!

DEAN.

As for your husband's supposed coldness, recollect that an ambassador, my dear, is, above all, a busy man, with duties of the highest and most delicate nature. You surely would not have him neglect these duties.

MIRIAM.

That is not what I mean.

DEAN.

As for the other charge against Sir Henry, it is a slander.

MIRIAM.

Will you make your own inquiries, and ascertain the truth or falsehood of the report?

DEAN.

Certainly not. Mine, I am happy to say, is the charity that thinketh no evil. Farewell, my beloved child. (*Mrs. Fortescue opens the door.*) I would not put such an insult upon one who has just furnished me with such practical proof of his large-hearted benevolence—(*pats his breast-pocket—aside*) and who will, no doubt, give additional proofs of it in the future.

MRS. F.

Allow me to show you out.

(*Exeunt the Dean and Mrs. Fortescue.*)

MIRIAM.

Can it be true? There may be some mistake. After all, Sir Henry is a gentleman, and no gentleman would make his wife a laughing-stock and a by-word among women! No, I must be perfectly sure. I will ask Sir Henry to take me with him. I will tell him that I have set my heart on going. If he says " Yes," then all this will be a mistake; if he says " No," then I shall know that it is true. What *shall* I do? I cannot stay here. I cannot see Mr. Sabine again. I will not trust myself.
(*Re-enter Sir Henry.*)

Oh, I'm so glad you've come back.

SIR H.

Yes?

MIRIAM.

I have been thinking over our late conversation—thinking it over very seriously—and I want you to take me with you.

SIR H.

My dear, you don't know what you are talking about. It is quite impossible.

MIRIAM.

Everybody expects me to go with you, and I *ought* to go.

SIR H.

The expectations of "everybody" are interesting, but I am afraid that I shall have to disappoint them.

MIRIAM.

You cannot be so unkind as to refuse me. I only beg that I may be allowed to take my proper position as your wife.

SIR H.

You already enjoy that position, and will be much more comfortable here in London. I have made every arrangement for your convenience, and have opened an account for you at Coutts's.

MIRIAM.

I am not asking for money, but for that consideration to which I am entitled.

SIR H.

And which, I trust, I have always shown you. It is in your own interest that I have decided not to ask you to share the anxieties and inconveniences of my ambassadorial exile.

MIRIAM.

It will be a pleasure to me to share your anxieties. Believe me, I am not acting from caprice. I have my own reasons for wishing to go with you.

SIR H.

And I have my own reasons for going alone.

MIRIAM.

What are they?

SIR H.

I must decline to be cross-examined.

MIRIAM.

I am your wife. I have a right to your confidence and to your society.

SIR H.

My confidence you possess in the fullest measure. As to my society, I had no idea that you found it so agreeable.

MIRIAM.

Husband—have you not one kind word for me? Can you not see that my heart is breaking? Let me go with you.

SIR H.

I have decided; is not that enough?

MIRIAM.

Sir Henry, your words chill me. You make love impossible.

SIR H.

You are very unreasonable, Lady Craven, and most ungrateful. You seem utterly to forget how much you and your father owe to me.

MIRIAM.

No, indeed, I remember it only too well; and I must congratulate you on your generosity in reminding me of my obligations.

SIR H.—(*Heedless of her interruption.*)

I have raised you from a position of obscurity to the very front rank of European society. I have given you everything for which a woman can wish.

MIRIAM.

Sir Henry, I will go to Constantinople. It is my right, and I insist upon it!

SIR H.

And I insist, for once in a way, upon being obeyed.

MIRIAM.

Sir Henry, listen to me before you finally decide. I dare not be left alone. I am afraid of myself. Will you not help me to do what is right?

SIR H.

My dear, you talk at random. I am not afraid of you. I have every confidence in you, and shall leave you with my own mind perfectly at rest.

MIRIAM.

Let me beg and implore of you to take me with you!

SIR H.

I cannot.

MIRIAM.

Why?

SIR H.

I *will* not!
(*Exit Sir H.*)

MIRIAM.—(*Dropping into seat rigidly.*)
Then it is true!

END OF ACT II.

ACT III.

SCENE.—LADY CRAVEN'S APARTMENT IN AN HOTEL AT NICE, OPENING ON A TERRACE OVER-LOOKING THE SEA.

(*Elise discovered putting the finishing touches to Mrs. Fortescue, who is in outdoor costume.*)

MRS. F.

There, Elise, I think that'll do. How do I look? (*Admiring herself in the glass.*)

ELISE.

Ravissante, madame. Madame is an artiste.

MRS. F.

Only in crayons, Elise. I never use any colour. That eyebrow is a work of art, I think—not overdone. I hate to see eyebrows the shape of a railway-arch.

ELISE.

It is perfection. Nature itself might take a wrinkle from madame.

MRS. F.

I wish to goodness Nature would. I could spare more than one. But Nature's like everybody else, fonder of giving wrinkles than taking them. How's the wind, Elise? Is it very rough?

ELISE.—(*At window.*)

There is none, madame. The sea is as smooth as glass.

MRS. F.

That's a good thing. The yacht won't rock about. I must confess I like to enjoy my supper in peace, and not to be chasing it all over the table.

ELISE.

Madame is going to sup on board Monsieur Sabine's yacht?

MRS. F.

Yes; we shall not be late.

ELISE.

How strange that Monsieur Sabine should happen to be at Nice.

MRS. F.

Strange! Not at all. No stranger than that Prince Balanikoff should be here.

ELISE.

Monsieur le Prince is everywhere.

MRS. F.

Everybody comes to the Riviera at this time of

the year; and Mr. Sabine is yachting in the Mediterranean.

(*Enter Lady Craven, in outdoor costume.*)

Mrs. F.—(*Addressing Lady Craven.*)

Ready, my dear? You look charming. Excuse me for monopolising Elise, but you have evidently not required her services.

Miriam.

Elise, my wrapper; I have mislaid it.

Elise.—(*Taking a wrapper from couch.*) Voilà!

Miriam.

What's it doing there?

Elise.

Thinking that after my lady had dismissed me this evening she might take a fancy to sit out on the terrace, I left it there, all ready. (*Both look at Elise, blankly.*) The nights just now are chilly, and my lady might take cold.

Miriam.—(*Coldly.*)

That will do. Thank you.

(*Exit Elise.*)

MRS. F.

What does she mean? Do you ever sit out on the terrace?

MIRIAM.

I did last night.

MRS. F.—(*Surprised.*)

Alone?

MIRIAM.

Mr. Sabine, whose rooms are next to ours, happened to be there, and we sat for a few moments talking. That is all.

MRS. F.

She must have seen you.

MIRIAM.

Evidently. I thought she was in bed and asleep.

MRS. F.

Then she was watching.

MIRIAM.

What does it matter? I have nothing to conceal.

MRS. F.

So you really *were* on the terrace last night with Mr. Sabine, after everyone had gone to bed.

MIRIAM.

I cannot see any harm in it.

Mrs. F.

How injudicious innocence is. A trifling *faux pas* is almost desirable to teach people discretion.

Miriam.

Mr. Sabine's having the next rooms to ours was quite an accident.

Mrs. F.

Such accidents ought to be avoided.

Miriam.

I cannot conceive what you are alarmed about.

Mrs. F.

Not I, my dear. It would take more than Mr. Sabine to frighten me! I'm not such an angel as you are, thank goodness! I shall be an angel quite soon enough. But *you* should be very careful of him, Miriam.

Miriam.

Well, it is useless inventing worries; one has quite enough real ones. I heard again on Monday from the Dean.

Mrs. F.

The Dean! I don't know how it is, my dear, but whenever I hear your reverend parent mentioned I always feel inclined to make a face. What does he want now?

Miriam.

Money, of course.

Mrs. F.

But he has fifteen hundred a year, besides all he can screw out of Sir Henry.

Miriam.

Why he should always be in difficulties I am at a loss to conceive.

Mrs. F.

I suppose the explanation is that good claret and burgundy are more expensive than bad whisky. Too much meditation, my dear, you may depend upon it.

Miriam.

His letters always contain a long string of excuses. His expenses are enormous; his account is overdrawn; the farmers who rent his glebe won't pay; nothing but resignation to the Divine will——

Mrs. F.

Oh, of course.

Miriam.

Sustains him. I am his rock, his corner-stone.

Mrs. F.

And will you answer by return of post?

MIRIAM.

How did you know?

MRS. F.

People who want money invariably want it by return of post.

MIRIAM.

P.S. "Bis dat qui cito dat!"

MRS. F.

Quite so. It wouldn't be complete without a bit of Latin.

MIRIAM.

Which he kindly translates for me: "She who gives quickly gives twice."

MRS. F.

And she who gives twice is asked thrice. I hope you didn't send him anything.

MIRIAM.

No. I am weary of his continual appeals; indeed, I've given up answering his letters.

(*Re-enter Elise.*)

ELISE.

Monsieur Sabine is here, my lady.

MIRIAM.

Oh, we are quite ready. Elise!

ELISE.

Yes, my lady.

MIRIAM.

You need not sit up.

ELISE.

No, my lady.

MIRIAM.

You were so late last night.
(*Exeunt Miriam and Mrs. Fortescue.*)

ELISE.

Sit up, indeed! It's you who will sit up, my lady! She fancies she can do without me, and that's just where she's been wrong. I've given her many a hint that I'd help her if she'd only make it worth my while; but she's pretended not to understand. I've never served such a woman before. Lady Golightly knew the value of a maid who had ideas. Lady Golightly must have had six or seven affairs on the tapis, and none of them knew there was anyone but themselves. Then there was my Lady Paddington. Oh, the delicate little affairs I managed for my Lady Paddington! and Madame la Duchesse also. A wink was as good as a nod to Madame la Duchesse. But there's no doing anything with my lady, or I wouldn't have written to Sir

Henry to let his Excellency know what's in the wind. Que voulez-vous ? Chacun pour soi !

(*Prince Balanikoff strolls along terrace, which runs alongside of hotel, smoking a cigarette; seeing Elise alone, he signals.*)

ELISE.

Monsieur le Prince !

PRINCE.

Alone, Mdlle. Elise ?

ELISE.

Yes, Monsieur le Prince. My lady and Madame Fortescue are both out.

PRINCE.

(*Entering.*) I am fortunate. It was you that I wanted to see.

ELISE.

Me ! Monsieur le Prince ?

PRINCE.

Can you spare a few moments ?

ELISE.

Certainly, your Highness. I have nothing to do.

PRINCE.

Pardon me, Mdlle. Elise, you have a great deal to do. You have the care of her ladyship's wardrobe, you have the custody of her ladyship's secrets, you have the charge of her ladyship's apartments, and, not least, the care of that most charming and interesting person, Mdlle. Elise.

ELISE.

Of course, Monsieur le Prince.

PRINCE.

Oh, yes, you have a great deal to do. Take my word for it.

ELISE.

Yes, monsieur le prince, I'll take your word for anything.

PRINCE.

Having so much to do, do you never forget anything?

ELISE.

Never!

PRINCE.

Nothing of importance, but now and then some little trifling thing?

ELISE.

I never forget *anything*, your Highness.

PRINCE.

I am sorry for that.

ELISE.

Sorry, Monsieur le Prince?

PRINCE.

However, there is no knowing what we can do till we try; and if she tried very hard, it might perhaps be possible even for Mdlle. Elise to forget some trifling detail.

ELISE.

Oh, if your Highness *wished* it!

PRINCE.

For instance, this window. It must be very difficult for a lady who has so much to think of to remember to fasten it every night.

ELISE.

I do it without thinking, your Highness.

PRINCE.

I wind up my watch without thinking, but sometimes I forget to wind it up.

ELISE.

I think I understand your Highness.

PRINCE.

If you fasten the window without thinking, could you not leave it unfastened *with* thinking?

ELISE.

Anyone might forget a little thing like that.

PRINCE.

Exactly.

ELISE.

Where is the harm? It will air the room.

PRINCE.

As you say, it will air the room.

ELISE.

And no one will come in.

PRINCE.

Nobody.

ELISE.

Why should they?

PRINCE.

Why should they?

ELISE.

I will remember to forget, your Highness.

PRINCE.

Mdlle. Elise, you are too intelligent for your position. It must be improved. (*Knock without.*) Some-one is here. Good-night. (*Going up, drops purse.*)

ELISE.

Bon soir, Monsieur le Prince! Monsieur le Prince! you've dropped something! (*Picks it up.*) Your portemonnaie.

PRINCE.—(*Stops and turns.*)

That is not mine.

ELISE.

Oh, but I saw it drop!

PRINCE.

It is not mine. It must be yours, Elise. (*Exit through the window.*)

ELISE.—(*Opens purse.*)

Deux cent francs! Il est gentil, Monsieur le Prince. (*Another knock.*)

DEAN.—(*Without.*)

May I come in?

ELISE.

Mon Dieu! C'est le bon père! (*Opens door.*) (*Enter the Dean.*)

DEAN.

Good-day to you, Elise. Is Lady Craven ill?

ELISE.

Ill! No, monsieur.

DEAN.

How you relieve my mind. Her correspondence with me ceased so abruptly, I feared some calamity had befallen her. Where is my darling child?

ELISE.

My lady is not at home. She has gone on Mr. Sabine's yacht.

DEAN.

Good gracious! What business has she on Mr. Sabine's yacht?

ELISE.

That is not my affair.

DEAN.

Good Heavens! What do you mean? You don't tell me that Mrs. Fortescue is not with her?

ELISE.—(*With contempt.*)

Madame Fortescue! Oh, ciel! it is Madame Fortescue that has led my lady into this folly.

DEAN.

Folly! Dear me, dear me! (*Aside.*) I must get to the bottom of this. Almsgiving is against my principles, but I think a shilling on such a momentous occasion—perhaps I'd better make it half-a-crown. (*Aloud.*) There are two francs. Now tell me what has Lady Craven been doing?

ELISE.

What has she *not* been doing? My lady and Monsieur Sabine they bill and coo like two turtle doves. He has taken rooms here at this very hotel, and next to my lady's, and they're out on the terrace together half the night.

DEAN.

Elise, you shock me! Dear, dear me! (*Aside.*) If this were to come to Sir Henry's ears, it might have the pernicious effect of drying up the wells of that excellent man's generosity. (*Aloud.*) Elise, you are quite right to take *me* into your confidence; but I implore you to say nothing to anybody else. I will reward you handsomely—most handsomely. You have already had an earnest of my liberality.

ELISE.—(*Aside.*)

Two francs!

DEAN.

A still tongue makes a wise head. Cultivate that silence which we are told is golden.

ELISE.

I am only a servant, monsieur; but I thought it my duty to acquaint her husband.

DEAN.

Great Heaven! You have told Sir Henry?

ELISE.

I have written to his Excellency to Constantinople.

DEAN.

Dear me! dear me! How very terrible! He may come here at any moment and discover everything.

ELISE.

Helas, monsieur! but I have done my duty.

DEAN.

Duty, indeed! How dare you do your duty? I mean, of course, how dare you interfere in matters that don't concern you? How could you blight the closing years of my unhappy life, and bring my grey hairs in sorrow to the grave?

SIR H.—(*Without.*)

Where is my wife? Out? It is false! I will see for myself!

ELISE.

Sir Henry!

DEAN.

All is over.

(*The door is flung violently open, and Sir Henry enters.*)

SIR H.

You here, St. Aubyn! What has brought *you* to Nice?

DEAN.

Alas, my dear Craven, we are both here upon the same painful errand.

SIR H.

You know, then, what has brought me from Constantinople?

DEAN.

Everything.

ELISE.

I have told his reverence.

SIR H.

Surely there's some mistake. Lady Craven cannot have so far forgotten what is due to her own dignity and my ambassadorial position.

DEAN.

Just what I said, Sir Henry. Let us humbly hope that Elise is mistaken.

ELISE.

But I'm *not* mistaken.

DEAN.

In common charity—without which cardinal virtue the rest are but sounding brass and a tinkling cymbal——

Sir H.

Silence, St. Aubyn. If Elise is right, this is a time for action, not for words.

Elise.

And I *am* right, Sir Henry. I can prove it.

Sir H.

Then I am a deceived, dishonoured man, the laughing-stock of Europe!

Dean.

My dear Craven, you have my deepest sympathy.

Elise.

Only last night, Sir Henry, my lady spent two or three hours on the terrace with Monsieur Sabine, when all the hotel was gone to bed, and to-night she is with him on his yacht. There is to be no one else there, except Madame Fortescue. I overheard him say so myself. (*Goes up.*)

Sir H.—(*To the Dean.*)

Did you ever hear of anything so disgraceful?

Dean.—(*Abandoning his daughter entirely.*)

A father naturally clings to his only child, however unworthy—that is poor human nature—but Miriam deserves no mercy.

Sir H.

There is nothing to be said in her defence. Explanations and excuses are out of the question. After to-night I will never meet her in this world again.

Dean.

My poor Craven, let us pray that Providence may soften this terrible blow.

Sir H.

I have my own honour to guard, and where that is concerned I am unflinching. Of course I shall divorce her, St. Aubyn; you must understand that.

Dean.

Of course, of course; I cannot take her part. Let me hope, however, my dear Craven, that *I* shall always retain your friendship.

Sir H.

Now, look here, St. Aubyn. Elise, just understand this. (*Elise comes down.*) I must have proof positive. My arrival must be kept secret. I will silence the hotel people; not a word must be breathed to Lady Craven. But you and I, St. Aubyn, must be near at hand; and Elise must summon us when the guilty pair least expect it.

ELISE.

I can manage everything, Sir Henry. You and his reverence had better go. I do not fancy that my lady will be late.

DEAN.

A very admirable suggestion. And indeed, I feel that I must really satisfy those physical cravings which so grotesquely assert themselves even in the supreme hours of grief.

ELISE.

Make haste, monsieur; I hear her.

SIR H.

Let us go at once.

ELISE.

By the balcony, or you will meet my lady on the stairs.

SIR H.

This way, St. Aubyn. Follow me.

DEAN.—(*Following.*)

I wonder if the table d'höte is over.

(*Exeunt Sir H. and the Dean by the window.*)

ELISE.

Ah, my poor mistress! I must be well paid for betraying her.

(*Re-enter Lady C., Mrs. Fortescue, and Mr. Sabine by door.*)

MIRIAM.

Anybody been, Elise?

ELISE.

Oh, no, my lady—personne.

MIRIAM.

I told you you need not sit up.

ELISE.

I did not mean to, but I fell asleep.

MRS. F.—(*Yawning.*)

That's what I shall do in a minute. I'm dead beat; so, if you will excuse me, I'll go to bed. Good-night, Mr. Sabine. There's not a boudoir in the world to compare for a moment with the saloon of your yacht. I never saw anything so lovely.

MR. S.

I'm glad you like it. (*Hand-shakings.*)

MIRIAM.

Good-night, dear. (*Kisses Mrs. Fortescue.*)

MRS. F.—(*Aside, to Lady C.*)

I shan't let you sit up long.

MIRIAM.

What nonsense!

MRS. F.

Come along, Elise. Help me to undress.
(*Exeunt Mrs. F. and Elise.*)

MR. S.

I hope you, too, have not fatigued yourself, Lady Craven?

MIRIAM.

Not in the least. I never felt better or brighter.

MR. S.

Suppose, when I had got you on board the yacht, you had begun to hear the engines throb and to feel the vessel vibrate, and found that we had weighed anchor and were under steam, and that I had carried you off?

MIRIAM.

You would never do such a thing. You are not a coward.

MR. S.—(*Laughing.*)

And yet, sometimes, one is sorely tempted.

MIRIAM.

Tempted to be treacherous?

MR. S.

Yes, when one's enemies set one the example. What duty does one owe to the burglar who breaks into one's house at night? Must one fight him with all the punctilio of the duello or hit him wherever one can?

MIRIAM.

I should think, hit him.

MR. S.

And yet one hesitates to strike even a burglar behind his back.

MIRIAM.

Pray, let us change the subject. It is getting rather late to talk about burglars. What was that?

(*Prince B. is seen passing the window.*)

MR. S.

Nothing. A footstep on the terrace—that was all. It is a favourite promenade in the evening. I'm afraid I have made you nervous.

MIRIAM.

Don't let us talk about such dreadful things.

MR. S.

Are they so dreadful? For my part I think the recognised professional criminal is a grossly ill-used individual. The criminals I would like to see punished are the mother who barters her daughter for position or an income, the father who sells her for the price of his debts, and the husband who pays it. These are the real criminals. In the fullest sense of the word, they take her life; but they have not the mercy to end it.

MIRIAM.

But if the daughter is a consenting party?

MR. S.

There is a very excellent principle of English law, that no contract for life is binding. Humanity is too short-sighted to foresee a life-time, and a wise principle protects it against itself. But alas! the law is like the rest of us: it does not act up to its principles; it makes an exception of marriage—the most important contract of all.

MIRIAM.

We are getting on dangerous ground.

MR. S.

On ground that is labelled "Dangerous," to prevent people finding it is firm.

MIRIAM.

Dangerous to me, if not to you, Mr. Sabine. The fates have always been against me, ever since I was a neglected, ill-dressed little child, wandering with broken boots along the Devonshire lanes. Now, I am the wife of a man who ill-treats me, who neglects me, who is unfaithful to me; but if he has forgotten *his* duty, I will not make that an excuse for forgetting mine. Good-night, Mr. Sabine. *(Rising.)*

MR. S.

I am to go? *(Rising.)*

MIRIAM.

Yes.

MR. S.

Till to-morrow?

MIRIAM.

May I ask a favour?

MR. S.

Anything in the world that I can grant, Lady Craven, is yours, with all my heart.

MIRIAM.

I only ask your friendship.

MR. S.

You have more than that.

MIRIAM.

And your assistance.

MR. S.

Whatever service I can render you, I shall esteem the most precious of all privileges.

MIRIAM.

Mr. Sabine, it is in your power to render me the greatest service a man can render a woman. I am going to put your professions to the test, but I feel sure they are sincere and will bear it. You say you are my friend. Let the beginning of our friendship be the end of our acquaintance. (*Pause.*) I have surprised you?

MR. S.

You have more than surprised me. I feel as if the earth had opened under my feet, and my life had fallen in ruins about my head. You cannot mean what you say.

MIRIAM.

I mean it, from the very bottom of my heart.

MR. S.

I am never to see you again?

MIRIAM.

Never.

MR. S.

Think to what you are condemning me.

MIRIAM.

I have thought—I know. I know, at least, to what I am condemning myself.

MR. S.

But *why* condemn yourself? Why condemn me?

MIRIAM.

Do not argue with me; help me to do what I am trying to do—my duty. It is very hard—harder for me than you. Do not set difficulties in my path, but help me.

MR. S.

By leaving you?

MIRIAM.

It is the only way.

MR. S.

See what it is you ask of me. In one brief moment of surprise to shatter the whole fabric of my life. Why should we not be friends? Can you not trust me?

MIRIAM.

I think I've given you sufficient proof of my regard and of my confidence. Be worthy of it. It will be true friendship! Go—without argument, without appeal; and, when we are far apart, I will think of you as the noblest man I have ever met, and I will pray for you as for him whom, unashamed and in all purity, I love best in the world.

MR. S.

Miriam, dearest! you have said enough. I know not whether I am the happiest man in all the world, or the most wretched; but rest assured that you shall never see my face again till your own voice has summoned me.

MIRIAM.

Heaven bless you, George! (*Giving her hand.*)

MR. S.—(*Kisses her hand.*)

Good-bye! (*Exit.*)

MIRIAM.

I am alone! alone in the wide world! Oh, why has God made duty so hard to be done? And where is the reward? None! none! I have done right, but am I happier? No; I am desolate.
(*Sinks on to couch.*)
(*Re-enter Elise, with dressing-gown.*)

ELISE.

Did my lady ring?

MIRIAM.

No; but I'm ready. (*Puts on dressing-gown.*) You can make up the room and go to bed. I shall not require you again. (*Elise makes up the door, etc., but not the window.*)

ELISE.

Good night, my lady.

MIRIAM.

Stay! You've forgotten the window.

ELISE.

Mon Dieu! que je suis bête! (*Pretends to fasten it.*)

MIRIAM.

Good night.

(*Exit Elise.*)

MIRIAM.

What a wasted life mine is! What an utterly aimless, hopeless future lies before me. I did not know how much I loved George Sabine till to-night. What a blind chance is life. It is terrible to think we two should never have met when love was possible, and *should* have met when it was too late. And how easy for Providence to have been kind! If it had only been otherwise, how changed my life would have been. What happiness, what joy, what bright and pleasant paths, instead of the dreary desert that lies before me. Ha! What is life? (*Enter Prince B., through window.*) What are you doing here? How did you enter?

PRINCE.

How I entered, dear Lady Craven, is not of so much consequence as is the fact that I am here.

MIRIAM.

And now that you are here, be good enough to go. Your presence here is an outrage.

PRINCE.

I shall not detain you long, Lady Craven. On the other hand, I have no intention of taking my departure until you have heard what I have to say.

MIRIAM.

I have no wish to hear anything. Go!

PRINCE.

All in good time.

MIRIAM.

Go, I say. I thought you were a gentleman.

PRINCE.—(*Coolly.*)

Listen to me. You are wasting your life, your bright days of youth and beauty. As for that young Englishman, no doubt he loves you—or thinks he does; but an Englishman's love at the best is worth very little. We Russians are much more serious in our passions and much more sincere.

MIRIAM.

I have no wish to prolong this discussion, and again I ask you to go. I refuse to listen to anything more.

PRINCE.

Dear lady, you wield an authority over me more potent than that of his Imperial Majesty himself. I will obey you in all things except this.

MIRIAM.

Prince Balanikoff, be good enough to understand, for once and for all, that our paths are entirely apart, and that under no possible circumstances could we be anything to each other. That is my answer, and I hope it is plain.

PRINCE.

You are condemning me to a death in life far more terrible than any death; more hopeless than even the deepest and darkest of Siberian mines. I hardly deserved this of you.

MIRIAM.

You have had my answer.

PRINCE.

You would find me very generous.

MIRIAM.

How dare you insult me so! (*Opens window.*) Go, without another word. (*Prince goes towards window, she away from it; he shuts the window, and sets his back against it, facing her.*)

PRINCE.

No, I will not go. Here I am—I stop here.

MIRIAM.—(*Rushes to door.*)

Ethel!

PRINCE.—(*Intercepting her, locks door.*)

MIRIAM.—(*Rushes to the other door.*)

Elise!

PRINCE.

Mdlle. Elise is my particular friend.

MIRIAM.—(*Rushes to window, Prince after her.*)

George! George! (*Prince overtakes her, and seizes her.*) Let me go! (*Struggling.*) George!

PRINCE.

You are strong, but I am stronger. (*Overpowering her.*) Say you will love me.

MIRIAM.

Coward! (*Strikes him.*) George! George!

(*Sabine dashes through window, hurls Prince to the ground, and carries Miriam swooning to the couch.*

PRINCE.—(*Picking himself up.*)

I will send my seconds to you in the morning. (*Exit.*)

MR. S.—(*With Miriam in his arms.*)

My darling! my darling!

(*Re-enter Elise in the moonlight, beckoning on Dean and Sir Henry.*)

END OF ACT III.

ACT IV.

(*Two years are supposed to have elapsed.*)

SCENE.—A CONSERVATORY LEADING INTO A BALL-ROOM AT LADY ASHWELL'S. (*Dance music heard off. Guests grouped about.*)

1ST GUEST.

Not dancing, Chetwynd?

2ND GUEST.

Not a dancing man. You've done your duty, as a soldier should.

1ST G.

My dear fellow, it's the finest exercise in the world. Three valses with old Lady Heaviside are as good as a season's hunting. I've worked off nearly half a stone already. (*Sits.*) Any news?

2ND G.

Only another batch of peerages, and a scratch lot they are. Now that they've used up the brewers, they don't seem to know where to turn.

1st G.

What can you expect? A Government that would make a peer of Sir Henry Craven would make one of anybody—unless he deserved it.

2nd G.

What a barefaced piece of business that was.

1st G.

Well, you see the fix they were in. If the old duffer hadn't been recalled from Constantinople we should have been at war with Russia by this time.

2nd G.

But why make him a peer?

1st G.

To keep him out of mischief. He couldn't keep out of it himself, and he couldn't keep his wife out of it either.

2nd G.

That was an unfortunate affair. Do you know, I was never quite satisfied with the evidence in that case.

1st G.

I think it was pretty conclusive. When a man finds his wife in another fellow's arms, in her own room, at midnight, he's a glutton for evidence if he wants any more.

2ND G.

But you forget her defence.

1ST G.

Oh, no, I don't. Some cock-and-bull story about a Russian Prince, uncorroborated in the smallest particular.

2ND G.

How *could* it be corroborated? The Russian was not likely to give evidence against himself, and the co-respondent was killed in the duel abroad. Why should they have fought unless there was something in it?

1ST G.

He must have loved the woman to have taken up her quarrel.

2ND G.

Anyhow, it was an infernal shame to grant that old humbug a divorce, when everybody knows he was living with another woman at Constantinople.

1ST G.

You mean everybody except the judge.

2ND G.

The innocence of our judges is phenomenal. They know nothing—except law; and I'm told that some of 'em don't know too much about that.

Directly a counsel is raised to the Bench he seems to take leave of his common sense.

1st G.

Well, you see, Mrs. Montressor wasn't in the pleadings, and it would have been travelling outside the record.

2nd G.

What's the Queen's Proctor for?

1st G.

I'm sure I don't know. I met him once. He's a nice, amiable old gentleman; but he can't do anything until somebody sets him in motion; and then he goes on doing nothing until somebody stops him.

2nd G.

Well, my sympathies are entirely with Lady Craven. She staked her case on her innocence, and was too proud to rely on a counter-charge. I never met the woman in my life, but I respect her for it. I wonder what's become of her?

1st G.

Heaven knows! What does become of women who have been through the Divorce Court?

2ND G.

I've often wondered. They can't all go on the stage.

(*Music stops. Enter various couples.*)

(*Move off.*)

(*Enter Lady Ashwell and Colonel Vandeleur.*)

LADY A.

Your friend is one of the most interesting men I've met for a very long time. I'm quite obliged to you for bringing him.

COL. V.

Yes, he's a very good fellow indeed. By the way, he has a very peculiar story.

LADY A.

Which of you men has not?

COL. V.—(*Laughing.*)

Or women either, for the matter of that. But George's story is stranger than any I have ever come across. He was engaged in a duel, was severely wounded, and was actually reported dead; and just when his heir-at-law was taking out letters of administration, he comes up smiling, as if nothing had happened.

LADY A.

How very extraordinary.

COL. V.

It turned out that he had been laid up in a foreign hospital, suffering from some complicated malady of the brain, and was unable to communicate with any of his family.

LADY A.

Well, it's a great mercy that he was not killed. He certainly looks none the worse for his experiences.

(*Enter Sabine and his partner. Sabine leaves his partner with her chaperon and comes up to Lady Ashwell.*)

MR. S.

Your floor is perfect, Lady Ashwell.

LADY A.

It is really very good of you to dance so energetically. You set an example to the young men of the present day, who appear too lazy to do anything except sit on the stairs until they are hungry enough to eat their supper.

MR. S.

It has always been my habit to throw as much energy as possible into the pursuit of the moment.

As a rule, I have found the benefit of this. Sometimes an exception occurs—now, for instance.

LADY A.

Yes.

MR. S.

There has been a task to which I have devoted myself, heart and soul, for the last three weeks; a task which brought me into this neighbourhood, and which, at any rate, has given me the pleasure of your acquaintance. Otherwise, unluckily for myself, it has been fruitless.

LADY A.

May I, without indiscretion, ask what it was?

MR. S.

The fact is that nearly twelve months ago I met with a serious accident—so serious indeed that it almost caused my death. I was abroad at the time, and I was taken to the hospital at the place where the accident occurred, nor did I leave it till a month ago. In the meantime I have lost sight of a dear friend to whom I was much attached. At first I could obtain no tidings whatever of her, then I got a clue which directed me to this part of the country, but now that I am here I do not seem to get much further in the enquiry.

Lady A.

You must let me know how I can help you.

Mr. S.

Thank you very much; but it is a long story, and I won't trouble you with it now. There is the music. I must find my partner.

(*Another dance. Sabine goes off with another partner. Colonel Vandeleur comes up.*)

Lady A.

What a delightful man your friend is. I seem to know his name, though I don't recollect anything about the duel. Where *can* I have heard it?

Col. V.

It was connected with some scandal; but most unjustly, as I happen to know.

Lady A.

Oh, I'll take your word for it. It doesn't do to go too deeply into these matters. And after all, what man is there who has not got into some kind of trouble? My boy—I call Ashwell my boy, though he is only my stepson—has hitherto kept out of all scrapes. I shall be glad, however, to see him married.

Col. V.

Isn't he rather young?

Lady A.

I married at seventeen myself; but, of course, it's different in the case of a man. And now that I am shortly to be married again, I shan't be able to look after Reggie.

Col. V.

I congratulate you on your courage. For my own part I never had the pluck to face matrimony.

Lady A.

Then you have got your Victoria Cross under false pretences.

(*Enter Lord Ashwell, with Miriam and Mrs. Fortescue.*)

Lord A.

Mother, this is Mrs. Gascoigne, whom I promised to introduce to you to-night. This, Mrs. Gascoigne, is my stepmother, Lady Ashwell.

Lady A.

I am delighted to meet you, Mrs. Gascoigne. My stepson has been loud in your praises, which, I now see, were more than justified.

Miriam.

It is very kind of you, Lady Ashwell, to say so.

Lord A.

Mrs. Fortescue—Lady Ashwell.

LADY A.

I am pleased to see you.

MRS. F.—(*Aside.*)

Humph! She don't look it.

LADY A.

Colonel Vandeleur—Mrs. Fortescue.

MRS. F.—(*Aside.*)

Wants to turn me over.

COL. V.

I have often heard Lord Ashwell speak of you Mrs. Fortescue. I feel that I know you already.

MRS. F.—(*Aside.*)

Oh, what a dear old man. (*Aloud.*) Has Lord Ashwell been loud in *my* praises?

COL. V.

Loud! Almost eloquent, But for all that, he has scarcely done justice to his theme.

MRS. F.

Oh, Colonel! (*Aside.*) I wonder if he's married? Might do worse.

COL. V.

But that is scarcely his fault. I once heard an enthusiast endeavour to describe the Venus of Milo.

Mrs. F.—(*Smiling.*)

The Venus of Milo? (*Aside.*) Am I as *décolletée* as that?

Col. V.

I will not attempt his description.

Mrs. F.

Thank you, very much.

Col. V.

Suffice it to say, he did not pourtray half her beauties.

Mrs. F.—(*Aside.*)

I should hope not.

Col. V.

I am not much of a dancer; but if you would let me be your pupil——

Mrs. F.

I shall be most happy to give you a lesson. (*Aside.*) Wicked old man—I like him.

Col. V.

For this dance I am engaged to Lady Ashwell; but if I might have the next——

Mrs. F.

I'm sure I shall be delighted.

Col. V.

Now, Lady Ashwell, may I have the pleasure?
(*Lady A. bows.*)
(*Exit with Lady Ashwell.*)

Mrs. F.—(*Aside.*)

What a dear old gentleman. I must find out if there's a Mrs. Vandeleur.

Lord A.

I told you, Mrs. Gascoigne, that you need not be afraid of my mother, and you see I was right.

Miriam.

Lady Ashwell is kindness itself; but I have been so long out of society that I feel quite nervous of entering it again.

Lord A.

I am sure society is indebted to me for restoring to it one so qualified to adorn it.

Mrs. F.

Only one?

Lord A.

Forgive me, Mrs. Fortescue. I did not see that you were there.

Mrs. F.

Oh, yes, I was there. I generally am.

Lord A.

I am sorry to say I am engaged for this dance, but I hope you will let me find you a partner.

Miriam.

Thank you; I prefer to sit out.

Lord A.

And you, Mrs. Fortescue?

Mrs. F.

Thanks, I'll reserve my energies.

Lord A.

I will be back as quickly as possible. (*Exit.*)

Mrs. F.

Well, here we are, Miriam, on our feet again. Wonderful, isn't it, how things shake down? It almost reconciles one to the scheme of creation.

Miriam.

Yes, we are here, Ethel; but I cannot help feeling that I, at least, am masquerading. How I wish now that you had never persuaded me to change my name. It was a mistake—almost a fraud.

Mrs. F.

My dear, it was imperative. How could you possibly face the world as Lady Craven? You might just as well go about with a label hung round your neck, " Heroine of the Craven Divorce Case. Three Shies a Penny."

MIRIAM.

But I was innocent.

MRS. F.

No matter, you lost; and the world never forgives a person who loses. I'm sure we're getting along splendidly. Only to think that a casual meeting at a cricket match should have introduced us into the best society in the county!

MIRIAM.

Under a false name.

MRS. F.

Never mind. If I know anything of human nature, you will be able to change it before long.

MIRIAM.

That is what I dread.

MRS. F.

Why should you? I'm sure Lord Ashwell is a most sensible and deserving young man, and will make you an excellent husband.

MIRIAM.

Hush, Ethel! Sometimes I grow weary of my life, and feel that I could do almost anything, even marry again. But the thought of George Sabine flashes through my mind like a streak of lightning through the night.

Mrs. F.—(*Aside.*)

Sabine again! He's worse than "The Lost Chord."

Miriam.

The world condemns Mr. Sabine; but how little it knows of the truth. The very man to whom, if the world is to be believed, I owe my ruin, is the one, the mere thought of whom strengthens and ennobles my whole nature. And to think it was through me he met his fate! If I had never crossed his path, he would be here still, true, strong, and valiant. Oh, my poor George, my heart breaks again.

Mrs. F.

Mr. Sabine was a very good sort—nobody admired him more than I did—though a more unresponsive male I never met in my life; but *he's* out of the question. Believe me, my dear Miriam, a husband in the flesh is worth ten lovers in the memory. If you take my advice, you will accept Lord Ashwell.

Miriam.

I wish I had told him the truth. I have told him

nothing that is untrue, but I have kept back from him the history of my unhappy past.

Mrs. F.

Miriam, you're a child. If you had any experience of life, you would know that one minute's truth is capable of making more mischief than a lifetime of falsehood can rectify. I shall tell Colonel Vandeleur just as much or little of *my* past as I think expedient. (*Dance ends.*)

Miriam.

Colonel Vandeleur?

Mrs. F.

My partner for the next dance. Here he is.

(*Enter various couples, amongst them Colonel Vandeleur and Lord Ashwell. Mrs. Fortescue goes off with Colonel, Lord Ashwell comes to Miriam.*)

(*Exeunt Colonel and Mrs. Fortescue.*)

Lord A.

I am soon back, Mrs. Gascoigne.

Miriam.—(*Aside.*)

The name seems to stab me.

Lord A.

And yet I can't tell you how long it has seemed.

MIRIAM.

Was your partner so uninteresting?

LORD A.

A duty dance, that's all. Now I have done my duty I mean to enjoy myself. You don't know how pleased I am to have you here to-night.

MIRIAM.

Shall we sit out this dance? We can talk so much better.
(*Another dance—Exeunt company.*)

LORD A.

And I have something particular to say to you.

MIRIAM.—(*Aside.*)

I must be the first to speak.

LORD A.

I have been waiting for this opportunity.

MIRIAM.

And I, too, Lord Ashwell. I wish to tell you something, something I meant to tell you long ago; but I have kept putting it off, as one does anything disagreeable.

LORD A.

Something disagreeable?

MIRIAM.

It is about myself.

LORD A.

Then it cannot be disagreeable.

MIRIAM.

I met you, quite casually, as you will remember; and I had no right, as well as no desire, to inflict my history upon you. But you have been so kind—in a few weeks we have become such friends—that I feel it is almost dishonourable to leave you under a false impression. There is a mystery in my past life which I cannot explain. It is nothing disgraceful to me; but a cruel combination of circumstances has forced me to assume a name that is not my own. I tell you this because I feel it to be a duty; but I tell it you in confidence, and implicit faith that you will keep my secret.

LORD A.

Miriam—if I may call you so—your secret is safe in my keeping. I will seek to know no more than you care to tell me; and, even without your assurance, I should have been quite certain that secret is in no way dishonourable. It would be false to say that you have not roused my curiosity, for everything that concerns *you* possesses the deepest interest for *me*. But I will ask no questions. I love you; yes, love you too much to doubt you. These are not empty words. Happily I am in a position to prove them. As an earnest of my love and my confidence —with this secret unspoken, with this mystery unexplained—I ask you, Miriam, to be my wife.

Miriam.

Lord Ashwell, you leave me no option. I must tell you a little more of my story. I once loved a man with all my heart and soul. That man is dead, or I should not be here. I can never love again as I loved *him*, and I will not be hypocrite enough to pretend that I can.

Lord A.

I had rather hold the second place in *your* heart, dearest Miriam, than the first in that of any other woman in the world. I have seen enough of the world to know that it is impossible for a woman such as you not to have been loved, not to have loved; I will be content with what affection you can give me, and I will hope for the rest in the future.

Miriam.

No, Lord Ashwell, it is impossible. My life has been wrecked; and it would be wicked of me, even out of mistaken kindness, to wreck another's.

LORD A.

You won't wreck my life, dearest Miriam. You will make me the happiest of men.

(*Re-enter Mrs. Fortescue and Lady Ashwell.*)

MRS. F.—(*Aside to Miriam.*)

The Colonel's coming on beautifully. I've ascertained he's a bachelor.

LORD A.

Mother, I won't conceal from you that I am in hope of inducing Mrs. Gascoigne to become my wife. May I not promise her that the kindness you have always shown to me, as a son, you will extend to her as a daughter?

MRS. F.—(*Aside.*)

Won in a canter! I shall only be second, after all!

LADY A.

Mrs. Gascoigne, I may say I am not altogether surprised. I have suspected Reginald's intentions for some little time, and I cannot tell you what a relief it is to me to find what good taste and judgment he has shown. I don't mind confessing now that I trembled a little at meeting you.

LORD A.

I told you, mother, there was nothing to be afraid of.

Lady A.

So I see now. But Reginald is so young, and there are so many designing women who somehow get admittance to society.

Mrs. F.—(*Aside.*)

Why does she look at *me*?

Lady A.

I didn't know who might have entangled him. Perhaps some heroine of the Divorce Court.

Lord A.—(*Seeing Miriam flinch.*)

Mother!

Lady A.

Forgive me, Mrs. Gascoigne. You have perfectly reassured me on that point.

Lord A.

I should have told you, Miriam, that if I were to marry without the consent of Lady Ashwell and my other guardian, a large portion of my money would be forfeited; and though money is not everything, it is an important factor in happiness.

Mrs. F.

Rather. (*Turns off—aside.*) Oh, dear! that slipped accidentally.

Lady A.

So far as I am concerned, you would have not only my good wishes, but my congratulations.

Miriam.

Lady Ashwell!

Lady A.

But at the same time, I think it only right to mention the matter to my future husband; for I, Mrs. Gascoigne, am about to be married.

Mrs. F.

I shan't be even second—a bad third.

Lady A.

I expect him this evening, and I venture to predict that you will be as charmed with *him* as he cannot fail to be with *you*.

Miriam.

I shall be delighted to make his acquaintance.

Lady A.

By reputation you must know him already. His name is indeed almost a household word.

Miriam.

May I ask what it is?

Lady A.

Certainly, dear.
(*Re-enter footman.*)

Foot.

The Dean of Southwick.
(*Enter Dean. Exit footman.*)

Miriam.—(*Turns back to Dean.*)

Ethel!

Mrs. F.—(*Aside to her.*)

My darling! Courage! If we are wrecked in port, let us go down all standing.

Lady A.

You have just come in time for supper.

Dean.—(*Aside.*)

I have not miscalculated.

Lady A.

I am so glad.

Dean.

Alas, Dorothea, I have already partaken of my frugal meal—a chop and a tomato. How truly it is written "Better a dinner of herbs——"

Lord A.

Mr. St. Aubyn.

DEAN.

Yes.

LORD A.

My mother wishes to introduce you to this lady.

LADY A.

Yes, dear Augustus, I am sure you will be charmed with her. Mrs. Gascoigne—the Dean of Southwick. (*Miriam turns.*)

DEAN.

Miriam!

LADY A.

You know her?

MIRIAM.

This, Lady Ashwell, is my father.

LADY A.

You have a daughter? You have never mentioned her.

DEAN.

Alas! I must plead guilty to a certain amount of charitable reticence. But surely a father may be forgiven for seeking to veil with the mantle of silence the shame of his erring child.

LORD A.

Shame?

MRS. F.

The shame is yours, Mr. St. Aubyn; and in every word you speak you publish it.

DEAN.

I am not addressing my remarks to you, madam.

LORD A.

Miriam, what does this mean?

DEAN.

Lord Ashwell, it is with the very deepest pain and grief that I am compelled to inform you that this, my unhappy daughter ——

MIRIAM.—(*Clasping her hands.*)

Father!

DEAN.

Is the divorced wife of a doting husband, whose heart she well-nigh broke by her duplicity and crime.

MRS. F.

How dare you speak of poor Miriam in that way?

DEAN.

As for this person, I should not like to say in your presence, Dorothea, what I think of *her*.

LADY A.

Mrs. Gascoigne, may I ask if you have any explanation to give, if you have anything to say?

MIRIAM.

I have nothing to say.

DEAN.

You exercise a very wise discretion. After what has passed, there is nothing to be said.

MIRIAM.—(*Turning on Dean.*)

How *dare* you assume my guilt?

DEAN.

Alas! it has been proved.

LORD A.

Do you deny it?

MIRIAM.

Yes, in the sight of Heaven! And you, my father, who know me, ought to be the first to believe me; and you, who sold me, ought to be the last to condemn me. You sold me for your own price, and you have received it. Now leave me, and go! As surely as I shall have to answer in this world and in the next, the guilt of all this misery rests with you.

MRS. F.

Quite right, Miriam.

DEAN.

May I beg of you, madam, to be silent?

Mrs. F.

Certainly not. Why should I? You want to do all the talking yourself.

(Dean lifts his hands, and turns aside, nearly running into footman, who is crossing stage with some liqueurs on salver. Dean takes one, back to audience. Exit footman.)

Lord A.

Miriam, you have denied this accusation, I believe you. Where I have given my love I give my confidence. All this shall make no difference with me. If my mother refuses her consent, I shall lose only money. Well, let the money go; I have *you* left; and I accept it as a sacred trust to strive to compensate you by my love as a husband for that of the father who withholds it.

Miriam.

Reginald, hush! I am not used to kindness.

Lady A.

But I forbid it. Reggie, are you mad? It would be social ruin.

Dean.

It would be moral sin. I speak as a dignitary of the Church.

LORD A.

Mr. Dean, I don't know very much about the Church or its dignitaries; but it seems to me it would be very much better if you had a little less dignity and a little more feeling—less charity on your lips and a great deal more in your heart. Were your daughter's offences ten times worse than you say, it is not for her father to proclaim them.

DEAN.—(*Meekly.*)

I did not speak as a father, but as a dignitary of the Church.

LADY A.

I am surprised at your language, Reginald. Mr. St. Aubyn is perfectly right. I certainly shall never give my consent to your marriage with this lady.

LORD A.

Mother, Miriam has not deceived me. She told me there was a mystery. I have perfect faith in her; and I shall appeal to my guardian, who is not a dignitary of the Church, but a man of the world, and a gentleman.

(*Re-enter footman.*)

FOOT.

Lord Delacour.

(*Enter Sir Henry Craven. Exit footman.*)

SIR H.

I must apologise for being——

MRS. F.

Sir Henry!

SIR H.

Gracious me! My wife! (*Picture.*)

LORD A.

Miriam, your wife?

LADY A.—(*to Dean.*)

Your daughter, Lady Craven?

DEAN.

It is too true.

SIR H.

What is she doing here? this woman who dishonoured my home—who dishonoured my name!

LORD A.

You need say no more. I am perfectly aware of the history of Lady Craven. It is public property. But I wish to make no mistake, and to do no injustice. Miriam, let me hear it from your lips. Is this the fact?

MIRIAM.

It is the fact that I was Lady Craven.

LORD A.

Have you no more to say?

MIRIAM.

I had intended to tell you everything. My life has had a history, and the history of a life cannot always be compressed into a few minutes of time.

LORD A.

I do not reproach you.

MIRIAM.

Good-bye, Lord Ashwell. You have acted throughout as a gentleman, and I shall carry to my grave the remembrance of your kindness.

LADY A.

Now, Lady Craven, I must ask you——

LORD A.

Hush, mother.

MIRIAM.

I am going. (*Moves a few steps, then falters, and is obliged to cling to some article of furniture for support.*)

MRS. F.

Good night, Lady Ashwell, and thank you very much for a most pleasant evening. Good-bye, Mr. St. Aubyn; I hope you will enjoy your supper. Ta, ta, Lord Delacour. (*Aside to him.*) My kindest regards to Mrs. Montressor.

DEAN.

Farewell, my child, and in sincere repentance may you yet find happiness.

MIRIAM.

My God! my God! To be iusulted so!
(*Falls half insensible.*)
(*Dance ends. Re-enter Omnes, and crowd round.*)

MRS. F.

Silence, you hypocrite; there is more goodness in your daughter's heart even than there is wickedness in yours. Will no one help her? Is there not a man amongst you?

MR. S.—(*Stepping forward.*)

If I can be of any service——

MRS. F.

George Sabine! (*Miriam springs up and turns.*)

MR. S.

Miriam! (*Miriam, recognising Mr. Sabine, gives one long, piercing shriek, and falls into his arms, sobbing convulsively.*) Miriam, look up. In presence of them all, I ask you for the right to love and guard you always. Will you not give it to me?

MIRIAM.

George!

MR. S.

My wife!

CURTAIN.

THE
Prisoner of Chiloane,

By WALLIS MACKAY.

ONE VOLUME.

With 80 Illustrations by the Author.

The WORLD says:—"A brightly written book."

MORNING POST:—"Bright and attractive."

The SATURDAY REVIEW:—"Mr. Mackay is as good with pencil as with pen."

The SCOTSMAN:—"Written in a bright, spirited style; and the illustrations are full of fun and movement."

The SPECTATOR:—"Much that is worth reading in Mr. Mackay's Book."

Foolscap Quarto, handsomely bound in Cloth, bevelled edges, 7s. 6d.

TRISCHLER & Co., LONDON.

LADY DELMAR.

By THOMAS TERRELL and T. L. WHITE.

This exciting Story of London life has already been dramatised by MR. SYDNEY GRUNDY.

The DAILY TELEGRAPH says:—"A remarkable novel." See also leading article on this dramatic story of human nature in *Daily Telegraph* of February 25th.

The DAILY NEWS:—"A complex story of life in London, with many exciting incidents."

TRUTH refers to "Lady Delmar" as "A striking novel" and "powerful."

PICCADILLY:—"'Lady Delmar' is distinctly a book to read; it is vivid with variety, culminating in interest, and original in treatment."

Handsomely Bound in Scarlet Cloth. 354 pp.
Crown 8vo, 3s. 6d.

ONE VOLUME.

TRISCHLER & Co., LONDON.

A MAIDEN FAIR TO SEE.

By F. C. PHILIPS and C. J. WILLS.

ILLUSTRATED BY G. A. STOREY, A.R.A

SCOTSMAN:—"This novel, both by its pictures (graceful drawings from the pencil of Mr. G. A. Storey) and the general style of its printing, suggests the book for young readers. The story is lifelike, humorous, and clever. Everybody who reads the story will enjoy its tenderness and quiet fun."

Foolscap quarto, beautifully bound, with gilt top, Six Shillings.

TRISCHLER & Co., LONDON.

 www.ingramcontent.com/pod-product-compliance
Lightning Source LLC
LaVergne TN
LVHW061216060426
835507LV00016B/1956